G

M000211099

Studies in Literature and Science
published in association with the Society for Literature and Science

MICHEL SERRES

Genesis

Translated by
Geneviève James and James Nielson

Ann Arbor
THE UNIVERSITY OF MICHIGAN PRESS

English translation copyright © by the University of Michigan 1995
Originally published in French as *Genèse* © Editions Grasset et Fasquelle 1982
All rights reserved
Published in the United States of America by
The University of Michigan Press
Manufactured in the United States of America
⊗ Printed on acid-free paper

A CIP catalogue record for this book is available from the British Library.

Library of Congress Cataloging-in-Publication Data

Serres, Michel.
   [Genèse. English]
   Genesis / Michel Serres : translated by Geneviève James and James
Nielson.
      p. cm. — (Studies in literature and science)
     Includes bibliographical references.
     ISBN 0-472-10592-2 (alk. paper)
     I. Title. II. Series.
   PQ2679.E679G413   1995
   844'.914—dc20   95-1555
   ISBN 0-472-08435-6 (pbk. : alk. paper)   CIP

The publisher is grateful for partial subvention for translation from the French
Ministry of Culture.

Acknowledgments

I am grateful for the help and support I have received from many individuals. My
thanks go foremost to Michel Serres. Since 1985, when this translation was initiated
in his graduate seminar at SUNY-Buffalo, he has never ceased to provide encourage-
ment. He has been most generous with his time, illuminating and explaining
difficult passages of his book. I would like also to thank my friend Kevin Longworth
and my colleague Raymond J. Clough for their time spent reviewing the manu-
script. I received invaluable assistance from my collaborator James Nielson during
our animated transcontinental e-mail discussions. I thank him for his perseverance
in uncovering the right acceptable English word for an impossible French pun.
Above all I thank my husband, William, for putting up with all the frustrations
engendered over the years with this incredible project.

                                              G.J.

I owe thanks to Paisley Livingston, who was responsible for my participation in
this book, and to Dominique Darmon, for a bit of consultation along the way.
Geneviève James has been an incredibly patient and magnanimous collaborator
and has drawn me back from blunder or excess again and again. Nyla Jean Matuk
kept me from going blind at the terminal, and Heathrow was, of course, a force to
be reckoned with.

                                              J.N.

For Annette Gruner Schlumberger
by way of affection and thanks

I confine myself to crying out, as the birds of the Capitol did in the old days, at the noise of the assailants.
  —Thomas Hobbes, dedicatory epistle to *Leviathan*

Contents

A Short Tall Tale

As I was sailing along that summer, under a dazzling sky, and drifting lazily in the wind and sun, I found myself, one fine morning, in the green and stagnant waters of the Sargasso Sea, at a mysterious spot where thousands of tiny sparks, all shapes and all colors, were glimmering crazily in the early morning light. Bearing off, I was dumbfounded to see an area almost two hundred and fifty acres square entirely populated by dancing bottles. There were countless little vessels, and each one no doubt bore its message; each had its freight and each had its buoyant little roll, ballasted with seawrack and rockery; each carried its hope and its despair. The coiling winds had compelled them all there, from far and near, from a thousand different quadrants. Their constant and perilous collisions made for an acute and cacophonic carillon, and this noise mounted heavenward, wafted to the horizon, it filled all space with giddy ecstasy.

The following night, a wide sargasso put me in danger of shipwreck. I had just about foundered. Swiftly I made a raft of some of the bottles, they worked well as floats and bladders, and thus did I make my way back to Bordeaux.

The Object of This Book

What I am offering to be sounded and perhaps fathomed in the following pages is a new object for philosophy.

~

A flight of screaming birds, a school of herring tearing through the water like a silken sheet, a cloud of chirping crickets, a booming whirlwind of mosquitos . . . crowds, packs, hordes on the move, and filling with their clamor, space; Leibniz called them aggregates, these objects, sets. He brought them to people's attention at least; even if he undervalued them by merely according them the status of a heap of stones; even if he kept them mum by classifying them under harmony.

We are fascinated by the unit; only a unity seems rational to us. We scorn the senses, because their information reaches us in bursts. We scorn the groupings of the world, and we scorn those of our bodies. For us they seem to enjoy a bit of the status of Being only when they are subsumed beneath a unity. Disaggregation and aggregation, as such, and without contradiction, are repugnant to us. Multiplicity, according to Leibniz, is only a semi-being. A cartload of bricks isn't a house. Unity dazzles on at least two counts: by its sum and by its division. That herd must be singular in its totality and it must also be made up of a given number of sheep or buffalo. We want a principle, a system, an integration, and we want elements, atoms, numbers. We want them, and we

2

make them. A single God, and identifiable individuals. The aggregate as such is not a well-formed object; it seems irrational to us. The arithmetic of whole numbers remains a secret foundation of our understanding; we're all Pythagorians. We think only in monadologies.

Nevertheless, we are as little sure of the one as of the multiple. We've never hit upon truly atomic, ultimate, indivisible terms that were not themselves, once again, composite. Not in the pure sciences and not in the worldly ones. The bottom always falls out of the quest for the elementary. The irreducibly individual recedes like the horizon, as our analysis advances. So then, knowledge returns to sets. But a global unity, all the same, remains scarcely accessible. We lose the particular; we've lost the world. We've obliterated the human being, the human being as something specific, as well as the human being in general. We've long ago given up the hope for a unitary knowledge; there's exceedingly little appearance of us living, thinking, or existing as a collectivity, under one law, indivisible. The universal now only appears as the local monstrously inflated. If reason demands a road that will lead us from the monads situated there, or from some locality or other, to a global monadology, we are forced to admit either that there is none or that it is without foreseeable end. So then, by giving up the multiple for the one, has reason given up its prey to chase a shadow? Reason makes use of concepts, under whose unities are sheltered multiplicities that are most often highly dispersed.

~

No doubt compelled by these disappointments, we've been obliged to substitute the search for relationships for the futile quest of beings. We have supposed this was a decisive and necessary step forward, but perhaps it was merely a detour. The element became a crossroads or nexus of relations, an exchange or cloverleaf, every system was limned as a network of connections. Locally, far from imagining a subset of two terms, only the line connecting them, an analogy or a distinction, was given emphasis. Globally, every theory of systems became a graph of either a simplex or a complex, all things being first of all situated in the depths of a black box. We despise contents, we administer flow charts. So then: the foregoing reasoning transports itself from particles to connections, without any major changes. Toward the end of his life, as we now know, Leibniz himself had already conceived a second monadology, a monadology of *vincula*—connections. Once more doubt now enters the picture. Are there any connections to begin with that can't be further analyzed? I have no proofs that the simple parasitic arrow, even, is a basic unit of relationship, truly undecomposable. I have believed as much, of course, and I still do; but I can't be sure. Who, in the end, and from the other side of the picture, can boast of having conceived a general system, of projecting or constructing a general system of communication or relation, as a universal network? What would be conveyed by it? and how? What harmony, what cacophony would come of it? Do we have any sort of an ear for hearing that kind of thing?

There is still the problem of finding out how relation is transformed into being, and being into relation—to which we will be returning.

~

Of old I told the example of the cloud, I told of the concept of a nebulous set, I sketched the fringe of the flame, fluctuating with time; I never attempted to conceive of the multiple as such, directly, without ever allowing unification to come to its aid. I am trying here to raise the brackets and parentheses, syntheses, whereby we shove multiplicities under unities. That is the object of this book: the multiple. Can I possibly speak of multiplicity itself without ever availing myself of the *concept?* I am attempting to open up certain black boxes where it is hidden away, some of the deep freezes in which it has been frozen, a few of the soundproof rooms where it remains mute. Hopelessly, I am attempting to open up Pandora's little casket.

Whence comes the flood, or pandemonium.

~

The multiple as such. Here's a set undefined by elements or boundaries. Locally, it is not individuated; globally, it is not summed up. So it's neither a flock, nor a school, nor a heap, nor a swarm, nor a herd, nor a pack. It is not an aggregate; it is not discrete. It's a bit viscous perhaps. A lake under the mist, the sea, a white plain, background noise, the murmur of a crowd, time.

I have no idea, or am only dimly aware, where its individual sites may be, I've no notion of its points, very little idea of its bearings. I have only the feeblest conception of its internal interactions, the lengthiness and entanglement of its connections and relations, only the vaguest idea of its environment. It invades the space or it fades out, takes a place, either gives it up or creates it, by its essentially unpredictable movement. Am I immersed in this multiple, am I, or am I not a part of it? Its edge a pseudopod takes me and leaves me, I hear the sound and I lose it, I have only fragmentary information on this multiplicity.

When we subsume multiplicity under unity, in a concept or a black box, we do not share in or parcel out information. Information is either total or null. We always assume that we don't know, or else that we know everything, yea or nay. Whereas commonly we know a bit, a meager amount, enough, quite a bit; there are various undulations, even in the hardest and most advanced sciences. We are confronted with or absorbed by the multiple where more than three fourths of our knowledge and actions are concerned. Without any principle of individuation, without any simple or easy integration, without any distinguishable concept, without any well-defined boundary between observer and observed, I can only define here an ordinary piece of information, of a given size in some way or another finite and subject to change; I will write once more, neither null nor total. When it's total or null, then unity appears, then comes a concept or a black box, evidence or ignorance, unreason or reason: the exceptions. We're neither gods, nor angels, nor stones, nor dead bodies.

The multiple as such, unhewn and little unified, is not an epistemological monster, but on the contrary the ordinary lot of situations, including that of the ordinary scholar, regular knowledge, everyday work, in short, our common object. May the aforesaid scientific knowledge strip off its arrogance, its magisterial, ecclesial drapery; may it leave off its martial aggressivity, the hateful claim of always being right; let it tell the truth; let it come down, pacified, toward common knowledge. Can it still do this, now that it has vanquished temporal power and reigns in its place, a clerisy? Is there any chance of it still wanting to celebrate a betrothal between its imperial reason and popular wisdom?

The object of this book is both a new one and a common one. We recognize it everywhere, yet reason still insists on ignoring it.

~

The multiple. Water, the sea. Perceptional bursts, inner and outer, how can they be told apart? How am I to tell, any environment I've entered, become immersed in, that this wood I'm confronted with doesn't go on forever, that I'll get to the edge of the forest some day? I can't see the trees of this forest. A murmur, seizing me, I can't master its source, its increase is out of my control. The noise, the background noise, that incessant hubbub, our signals, our messages, our speech and our words are but a fleeting high surf, over its perpetual swell. Beyond one white plain, there is another white plain, after this dune, a second dune, past a branch of the Ganges delta, a hundred more branches of the Ganges I can't get across. The atmosphere we breathe and hatred, the hate in which we bathe, the hatred that never leaves the we, the hate that separates and joins, that syrupy hate. The collective with its inaccessible edges that we try to conceive with some objectivity. The crowd, fervent or ritual, the common crowd of the centers or the inflamed rabble when it runs wild. Life, the mantle of life that covers me, the generative field of life in which I am only a singularity alive. A certain death at an uncertain hour. Life, my life, work, my work, my labor, my project, this desert with or without a masterpiece, with or without any Mount Carmel summit. Sea, forest, rumor, noise, society, life, works and days, all common multiples; we can hardly say they are objects, yet require a new way of thinking. I'm trying to think the multiple as such, to let it waft along without arresting it through unity, to let it go, as it is, at its own pace. A thousand slack algaes at the bottom of the sea.

I'm attempting to think time. I'm well aware that time has no unity, no moment, no instant, no beginning, no end, and that I have no knowledge of its eternal completeness. For all the times that I've been able to tell, all of them were unities. I am now attempting to rethink time as a pure multiplicity.

Thus, perhaps, can history be born. History is in the midst of these hazy midsts, commonly lived, uneasily thought, it is, as it happens, information neither total nor null, without a clear-cut boundary between the observer and the observed. Like the ob-

server, it is full of sound and fury. A meditation on pure multiplicity, this book, is seeking, beyond the sea, the plain, the branch of
the river—noise, hate, time—seeking a philosophy of history. The
multiple is the object of this book and history is its goal.

~

These are objects I seem to live through more than view. I think I
pick up noises from them more than I see them, touch them, or
conceive them. I hear without clear frontiers, without divining an
isolated source, hearing is better at integrating than analyzing, the
ear knows how to lose track. By the ear, of course, I hear: temple,
drum, pavilion, but also my entire body and the whole of my skin.
We are immersed in sound just as we are immersed in air and
light, we are caught up willy-nilly in its hurly-burly. We breathe
background noise, the taut and tenuous agitation at the bottom
of the world, through all our pores and papillae, we collect within
us the noise of organization, a hot flame and a dance of integers.
My acouphenes, a mad murmur, tense and constant in hearing,
speak to me of my ashes, perhaps, the ones whence I came, the
ones to which I will return. Background noise is the ground of our
perception, absolutely uninterrupted, it is our perennial suste-
nance, the element of the software of all our logic. It is the residue
and the cesspool of our messages. No life without heat, no matter,
neither; no warmth without air, no logos without noise, either.
Noise is the basic element of the software of all our logic, or it is
to the logos what matter used to be to form. Noise is the background of information, the material of that form.

~

Hearing is a model of understanding. It is still active and deep
when our gaze has gone hazy or gone to sleep. It is continuous
while the other senses are intermittent. I hear and I understand,
blindly, when evidence has vanished and intuition has faded out:
they're the exceptions.
    I begin to fathom the sound and the fury, of the world and of
history: the *noise*.[1]

~

The multiple had been thought, perhaps, but it hadn't been sounded.

Les Treilles, July 1981

1

La Belle Noiseuse

TREE
  NOISE
    SEA NOISE
      PROTEUS
        DOUBLE DOUBT
          WORK
            ICHNOGRAPHY
              THE FOOT
                THE POSSIBLE
                  THE APPARITION OF FORMS

This that I'll be telling happened at the beginning of the seventeenth century, a time of quarrels and to-dos, whence came that body of geniuses, reason, beauty, we admire today.

This that I'll be telling, and that Balzac relates, couldn't happen, never took place. One of the names in it is a French one, another name in it is Flemish, and the third is German, though imaginary. Has anyone ever yet seen, in this history, the meeting of the real and the symbol? Poussin and Porbus no more knew Frenhofer than they knew his canvas.

The Unknown Masterpiece is a fake. This takes place in a locationless location, is from the pen of a nameless author, tells a story beyond time. No, there's nothing behind it, not even a woman. This masterpiece may be improbable or it may be impossible, but it isn't unknown and there is nothing to know. Or else: is there something still, once more, altogether anew to know?

Tree

Balzac depicts three painters, contemporaries and successors. This all took place during dark days when only headstrong souls without hope keep the sacred flame, in the bare certainty that it must continue to burn. A tree passes through them, a tree of creation, a family tree, a tree of life, a tree of knowledge. The child Poussin at the foot of the tree. Porbus, mature, in the middle of the trunk, and the old man Frenhofer, lost and crowned in the golden boughs. Or else—I'm not sure which way it points—the child Poussin in the green boughs, Porbus at the main branching, and the old painter with the diabolical look in the deep shade at the roots—looking like he'd emerged from the dark shadows of Rembrandt. As I am telling the tale, and as Balzac is telling it, and as the old man paints the second man's canvas under the dazzled gaze of the third, an invisible organist plays the Eastertide motet *O Filii*. Music. Sons and daughters, rejoice, the king of heaven was snatched from death this night. What resurrection can we hope for, in these dark times, what murdered son of this trinity is reborn to day, to the light of day? What is to be born from these days of wrath and flashing outbursts?

~

Nicolas Poussin is still young, Nicolas doesn't know that he is or that he will be Poussin, has such a thing ever been known, recognized, hoped for? He lives in his garret, in poverty, with Gillette, a perfect beauty. Go to Turkey, Greece, wherever, and you won't find a comparable one. Poussin is beginning, he begins before our very eyes, before the eyes of Porbus and Frenhofer, he executes a brisk copy of Mary the Egyptian, with sketches of red. Father and grandfather are excited, Nicolas is invited in.

Porbus, mature, lives in his studio, with his *Egyptian Marie*, a masterpiece intended for Marie de Medicis. The young talent sketches this woman, the old man touches her up, brings her to life, back to life. The genealogy is very exact in terms of descent. Mabuse, absent, gone without a disciple, bequeathed to the old master before us the technique of life, the master applies in little dabs to the breast, to the limbs, to the background, onto Porbus's canvas, and the youth copies it in ruddy strokes, a monochrome sketch. Life descends, disappears, there's a direction to the tree, from the old man to the young one.

Nicolas lives with Gillette, a perfect beauty. Porbus lives with Mary, an image that lives only in spots and which in spots does not. A mixed set. Porbus is at the top, he's going to be on the descent, Marie de Medicis has just left him for Rubens. He's wavering, unsure, in the middle: Marie is here a woman and there a statue, here stiff as a cadaver, there blazingly radiant. A motley escutcheon. Frenhofer lives with Catherine Lescault, a courtesan, the *"belle noiseuse"*—the beautiful clamorer or the querulous beauty—who doesn't exist; there's nothing on his canvas but a messy medley of colors. Life is on the ascent, it is gaining, the tree runs the other direction.

The tree runs in one direction for the men, where the brush loses, through time, its power. It flows back in the opposite direction for the women, where beauty wins, through time, its tranquil presence. Time flows in one direction for the maker, it flows the opposite way for the model. Nicolas, with his sketches, lives alongside being itself, the old creator has lost this. Porbus is in the middle, disturbed, uncertain and wavering. His painting fluctuates and doubts, it crosses over the river of time.

I no longer know the point of the tree, which way it points, in this crossing, I don't know the sense of time, where the rivers are headed. While Gillette stands absolutely beautiful and forsaken, naked, in the corner of the studio, all eyes look with envy upon the wall of blind matter. The model says: I love you and I hate you, I despise you and admire you. Nicolas has just reached Porbus's maturity, after the blinding short-circuit of the genius old man and the beautiful girl. Let us attempt to get the sense of time again.

~

I'll begin again, slowly. The three men form a sequence, following the order of Mabuse, as one says that priests are ordained, time and time again, following the order of Melchizedik. The three painters follow one another, following the order of representation, Mabuse's proper name can't fool us. All three of them have turned to their own picture, while, behind them, forgotten, naked, the beauty weeps. The three women, for their part, follow one another in the order of being. Not according to the order of appearance, but according to the scale of beings. Catherine is destroyed and entombed, Mary, wavering, existing and not existing, is about to cross the river of mortality; Gillette, in love, is exploding with life and nativity. An image lost in the arrangement, dissolved; half-corpse, half-mortal, half-statue, half-mobility; heat that is naive and there, present. The tree of beings comes out of the painting, the tree of representations, obviously, goes into it. Why is it that these two times, two directions, two scales, two trees form crosses?

Is this a quite ancient, quite absurd way of thinking?

Noise

We did not look carefully at the canvases. Yet Balzac makes them manifest. Let us try to forget for a moment the facile stunt where what he shows us shows us in turn a painting, which shows us what... Let us keep the sacred fire, in these dark hours. Let the green serge drapery clothe Catherine, so very naked under her thick wall of jeweled colors. She looks like the vestal Tarpeia, buried under the precious bracelets of the Sabine warriors. Did you or didn't you see Catherine? The painter wished not to let her be seen, destroyed.

Catherine Lescault, the river-christened courtesan, is here baptized *La Belle Noiseuse.*[1] I think I know who the *belle noiseuse* is, the querulous beauty, the noisemaker. This word *noise* crosses the seas. Across the Channel or the Saint Laurence seaway, behold how the *noise* divides itself. In Old French it used to mean: noise, uproar and wrangling; English borrowed the sound from us; we keep only the fury. In French we use it so seldom that you could say, apparently, that our language had been cleansed of this "noise." Could French perhaps have become a prim and proper language of precise communication, a fair and measured pair of scales for jurists and diplomats, exact, draftsmanlike, unshaky, slightly frozen, a clear arterial unobstructed by embolus, through having chased away a great many *belles noiseuses?* Through becoming largely free from stormy weather, sound and fury? It is true, we have forgotten *noise.* I am trying to remember it; mending for a moment the tear between the two tongues, the deep sea one and the one from the frost-covered lake. I mean to make a ruckus [*chercher noise*] in the midst of these dividing waters.

Sea Noise

There, precisely, is the origin. *Noise* and nausea, *noise* and the nautical, *noise* and navy belong to the same family. We mustn't be surprised. We never hear what we call background noise so well as we do at the seaside. That placid or vehement uproar seems established there for all eternity. In the strict horizontal of it all, stable, unstable cascades are endlessly trading. Space is assailed, as a whole, by the murmur; we are utterly taken over by this same murmuring. This restlessness is within hearing, just shy of definite signals, just shy of silence. The silence of the sea is mere appearance. Background noise may well be the ground of our being. It may be that our being is not at rest, it may be that it is not in motion, it may be that our being is disturbed. The background noise never ceases; it is limitless, continuous, unending, unchanging. It has itself no background, no contradictory. How much noise must be made to silence noise? And what terrible fury puts fury in order? Noise cannot be a phenomenon; every phenomenon is separated from it, a silhouette on a backdrop, like a beacon against the fog, as every message, every cry, every call, every signal must be separated from the hubbub that occupies silence, in order to be, to be perceived, to be known, to be exchanged. As soon as a phenomenon appears, it leaves the noise; as soon as a form looms up or pokes through, it reveals itself by veiling noise. So noise is not a matter of phenomenology, so it is a matter of being itself. It settles in subjects as well as in objects, in hearing as well as in space, in the observers as well as in the observed, it moves through the means and the tools of observation, whether material or logicial, hardware or software, constructed channels or languages; it is part of the in-itself, part of the for-itself; it cuts across the oldest and surest philosophical divisions, yes, noise is metaphysical. It is the complement to physics, in the broadest sense. One hears its subliminal huffing and soughing on the high seas.

Background noise is becoming one of the objects of metaphysics. It is at the boundaries of physics, and physics is bathed in it, it lies under the cuttings of all phenomena, a proteus taking on any shape, the matter and flesh of manifestations.

The *noise*—intermittence and turbulence—quarrel and racket—this sea *noise* is the originating rumor and murmuring, the original hate. We hear it on the high seas.

Proteus

Proteus—the god of the sea, a minor and marginal god, nonetheless a god of the first water, a god whose name stands at the beginning—is the shepherd who tends the oceanic flocks in the prairies of Poseidon. He dwells in the waters round the isle of Pharos, near the mouth of the Nile, Pharos, bearer of the first Beacon, Pharos, the fire that sheds light, standing out against a misty background, yet whose name means canvas, sail, veil: revealing, re-veiling. For instance, it is the pharos that Penelope weaves and unweaves. In these places of truth, Proteus undergoes metamorphoses: he is animal, he can be element, water, or fire. He's inert, he's alive. He's under the beam of the beacon, he's under the veil. He knows. He's a prophet, he possesses the gift of prophecy, but refuses to answer questions. He contains all information, admits no information. He's the possible, he's chaos, he's cloud, he's background noise. He hides his answers under the endlessness of information. When, for instance, his daughter consults him: he becomes a lion, he becomes a snake, he becomes a panther, a boar, water, a tree, and I don't know what all. The chain that steadies the phenomenal must be found. Chained, motionless, Proteus speaks, answers his daughter. Crafty, but not a trickster. At last he has found his master in physics. Physics is Proteus chained. Background noise is this Proteus badly bound. The sea breaking free. Behold a myth, barely a myth, which grants us an epistemology that is globally accurate, locally rich and detailed. It doesn't grant it in a language all rigor-worn, but through a channel full of noise, murmuring, and images.

What the narrative of Proteus does not tell is the relationship between chaos and form. Who is Proteus when he is no longer water and not yet a panther or a boar? What the narrative says, on the contrary, is that each metamorphosis or phenomenon is an answer to questions, an answer and the absence of an answer to the questioning. Locally responsive and globally sub rosa. Each appearance—each experience—is a lighthouse-pharos and a pharos-veil, a flash of illumination and a blackout of occultation. Proteus conceals information under the vast abundance of information, a straw in a haystack full of straw. He has an answer for everything; he says nothing. And it is this nothingness that matters. To physics, then, I now prefer metaphysics. The latter is free of Proteus's chains.

Proteus's intermediary states are sea sounds as they are bounding, abounding, unbounding. The *belle noiseuse* is restless. And all at once I know, at sea, who the *belle noiseuse* is. We have to recognize her in the midst of the colored wall of the swell, among the smacking and frothing of forms and tones, the breaking forth of the element divided against itself. Porbus and Poussin never had the right to look at the canvas. And when the old man unveils it, they can't make anything of it. They examine the painting, from left and from right, from right in front, alternately from below and from above. Points of view, phenomena. Fools. And they turn their back on the beautiful, living young woman. Fools. Porbus and Poussin did not see the *belle noiseuse,* and they consider the old man who sees her a fool. Balzac too thinks he is crazy. I guess I'm old enough now to see her. So many mariners never saw anything in the *noise* of the sea; only felt nauseous, organisms teeming with the sound and the fury, like the heaving gray itself; so many only felt the sad nausea over the root of the tree, an avatar of Proteus, so many only experienced phenomenological nausea, so many never saw the *belle noiseuse,* a naked Aphrodite resplendent in her beauty, rising fresh from the troubled waters, as the model Gillette who comes forth naive and aborning from the chaotic canvas of the dying old master. Who cut his brush dripping with color to throw it on the seascape and give rise to Aphrodite?

Double Doubt

Poussin sketches with an exact, precise, rapid stroke. Poussin has no doubt; Gillette is there, alive. The edge of his flying stroke is

Taylor smooth, almost infinitely smooth. No need to trim it, it is as smooth-skinned as youth. It is rational: no stubble, no hair, no filth or dirt. The neat edge does not hesitate over its definition.

Porbus, mature, in his prime, in his mastery, indeed—in his royalty, doubts. Everywhere his portrait is double: here a painting, there a drawing, here Flemish, there Italian, here dry, there burning, incandescent, here a cadaverish statue, there alive, enough to fool the emperor. Everywhere his painting is double and everywhere doubt, a mix. His stroke wavers a little, hesitates, fluctuates, indecisive. What path will my life choose? La Medicis will soon leave him for Rubens, a mountain of rose and vermilion. Double doubt spreads all over, at all points, at all sites of edge and boundary, at all parts of the body, in all moments of life itself. Marie does not know whether she is going to cross the water, the boatman himself is full of this indecision, the river fluctuates, and the painter hesitates. Doubt: having two movements and two intentions, two goals and two conducts, leaving the branching there before you, leaving stubble on the stroke, leaving the bifurcation cleft.

From Poussin to Porbus, the simple becomes double. From the student to the master, decision is raised, suspended. The climb toward mastery is a promotion to anxiety and absence of peace. The first stroke goes awry. The thundering passage, the flashing edge are a-tremble. The bankside undulates. Mastery probably does come down to this pathetic doubt.

Time rising from the child toward maturity or from apprenticeship to craftsmanship does not run along the single track replay, decision, rectitude. I waited until I had reached an age that was so ripe, that I could hope for no other one after it . . . so now I've got to act, he says. Descartes doubts, he goes back in time, toward father Montaigne, his hesitant questioning. Descartes doubts little, he recovers, thanks to God, the smooth and decisive simplicity of certitude. He prunes the bifurcation, he trims the stroke and gets back on the right track. Old Frenhofer, heroic, has tasted the simplicities of perfection, you need only see what he calls his studies; but still more heroic, he climbs back to this side of Porbus's double doubt and makes it abound. He does not stray back— God Almighty behind him—into the valley of certitudes. The word *doubt* is now at the center of all his sentences; it accompanies all his words, like a double shadow, it sends his brush awry. His brush multiplies branches and bifurcations. He climbs again the thalweg of the river where Marie the Egyptian wavered, where the boatman fluctuated, he climbs again the *chreod,* the course, the fall of the Scheldt [*l'Escaut*]. The confluence is no longer a low synthesis but a high opening that leads, further upstream, to other openings. The downstream course, the worn-out path, the slope, the chreod, run, from upstream confluences to downstream confluences, toward synthesis and the unitary. The upstream course, double doubt wavering to begin with, multiplies its bifurcations like a seven-armed candelabrum, like a full bouquet, a bush, an arborescence, a head of hair, a refined network of veins and fibrils, an endless network of doubts, anxieties. The old master did not prune, he did not trim his doubt, he let the possible burgeon and abound.

He goes back up the slope, goes back in time, giddily upwards, he rejuvenates. The productive man is born old and dies young. The productive man turns time around. You will recognize a thinker by the way he goes from truth to possibilities. As life goes from repetition to negentropy. Mortal time runs along the tree of the river, down, work runs along the straight tree, runs up. That tree, alive, teems, bushes, abounds in profusion.

I did not fix the lineaments, he would say, I scattered over the lineaments a cloud of blond and warm half-tints making it impossible to put one's finger on precisely the place where the outlines meet the background. From close up this work seems cottony, appears to lack precision, but two steps back everything firms up, becomes fixed and stands out . . . Yet, still I have doubts.

The old madman is on the way to the unknown secret of life.

~

The adult Descartes, doubts removed, shows the smooth and straight way. It is the best one, it is optimal, it is calculated through superlatives, it is the lowest one. At the low point, convergence, the tree appears analytical, simply. It is true that this path is universal. So much is gained there, gained there so often, that it would be foolish to take a different one. Reason rushes forth, analytical, toward the lower, universal confluences of synthesis.

Against the grain of Hegel, so young, or so old, against the grain of Descartes the adult, we can try to rejuvenate by going back up this chreod that remains short of Montaigne ...

Work

The masterwork is unknown, only the work is known, knowable. The master is the head, the capital, the reserve, the stock and the source, the beginning, the bounty. It lies in the intermediary interstices between manifestations of work. No one can produce a work without laboring in this sheer sheeting cascade from which there now and then arises a form. One must swim in language and sink, as though lost, in its noise, if a proof or a poem that is dense is to be born. The work is made of forms, the masterwork is a formless fount of forms, the work is made of time, the masterwork is the source of times, the work is a confident chord, the masterwork trembles with noise. He who does not hear this noise has never composed any sonatas. The masterwork never stops rustling and calling. Everything can be found in this matrix, nothing is in the matrix; one could call it smooth, one could call it chaotic, a laminar waterfall or clouds storm-crossed, a crowd. What are called phenomena alone are known and knowable, avatars of a secret remote proteus emerge from the clamorous sea. Visible and beautiful are the dispersed tableaux; beneath the green serge veil, lies the well. Empty, full, will we ever know? When there is an infinity of dispersed information in the well, it is really the same well as if it were devoid of information.

The *belle noiseuse* is not a picture, it is the *noise* of beauty, the naked multiple, the numerous sea, from which a beautiful Aphrodite is born, or isn't born, accordingly. We always see Venus without the sea; or the sea without Venus, we never see physics emerging, anadyomene, from metaphysics. Formed phenomenal information gets free from the chaotic background noise, the knowable and the known are born from that unknown.

The work, through profiles, snapshots, Protean shapes, emerges from the perturbation, from the noisy turbulent sea around the island of Pharos, flashes, occultations, of the protophare. Without this pileup, without this unknowable ichnography, there are no profiles, no work. It is necessary to dare to unveil the ichnography, at times, the one we always carry with us, in the dark, and as though secreted, in a receded nook, under a veil. Like a palette.

Ichnography

The painting revealed at the end of the narrative is the ichnography. *La Belle Noiseuse* is not a painting, not a representation, not a work, it is the master, the wellspring, the black box that comprises, implicates, envelops, in other words: buries all profiles, all appearances, all representations, and finally the work itself.

Poussin, Porbus run up to the canvas, move away, lean forward, from right to left, top to bottom, they look for a scenography, as is customary. And situate themselves at a vantage point in order to get an oblique profile. Fools. With luck, they will find a spot from which a straightforward form will appear. Scenography, orthography. And seek, as is normal, a place for a phenomenon, a space and an avatar, a cell and a science. A representation.

And thus they do not see the ichnography.

Balzac saw the ichnography. I think he knew he saw it. Since he signed it with its name. But like Frenhofer, like Mabuse, he bashfully masked it. And the ichnography remained unknown.

Leibniz never saw the ichnography. He probably proved that it was invisible. He never knew it, he proved that it is unknowable.

Once more, what is the ichnography? It is the ensemble of possible profiles, the sum of horizons. Ichnography is what is possible, or knowable, or producible, it is the phenomenological wellspring, the pit. It is the complete chain of metamorphoses of the sea god Proteus, it is Proteus himself.

It is thus inaccessible. We are tied down to a spot, our limitation, our definition is our point of view, we are chained to scenographies. Leibniz would say: the flat projection is in God and for Him.

Leibniz never saw the ichnography, but he knew where it was. This flat projection is in God, it is God. He did have an idea, though, about this flat projection, a rational idea. The intellection of God, as a sum of true ideas or as a reservoir of possibilities, as a sum of the atoms or seeds of truth, as the integral ultimately, is also rational. It would no doubt have seemed absurd to the old master for rationality in its totality not to be rational. There exists a path from the local to the global, even if our infirmity deprives us for all eternity of the ability to proceed along it. Better still, noise, the *noise*, false harmony be it in music, voice or hatred, are matters of simple local effects. *Noise*—shouts and war—has the same range of meaning, only symmetrical to harmony—song and peace. A noisy philosophy would be the shadow of Leibnizianism. The latter relegates it to little departments. In the seventeenth century, you see, hatred *was* limited and squabbling *was* confined. The uproar, the murmur of the sea, the generalized confused battle, nausea, are not avoided, but, once again, are the effect of narrowness or limited perceptions. Our body is constructed so as to integrate the buckshot drab, the blaring waterfall folderol, which would otherwise leave us dazed. Chaos, noise, nausea co-exist, only relegated to an oblivion that resembles repression and that is called apperception: unconsciousness. Often we are drowned in this confused minuteness. The more one ascends, on the contrary, the flights of integration, the more the rational rationalizes itself. Just as our body integrates the *noise* of minute perceptions into sensible signals, so does̄ God integrate in absolute knowledge, in white light, the relative *noise* of our right, flighty thinking. Harmony removes itself from noise, irenism removes itself from fury, as the universal removes itself from the local, the same distance: huge, infinite, measurable. Ichnography, then, should be pure. Smooth, white, unified like a perfect chord. Entering my old master Leibniz's abode, as a ward, and getting, I believe, as far as his studio, I had had only the beautiful Irene to contemplate. That picture of *The Production of Things* where the confused blob of color is only a local cover-up.

Leibniz was perceptive enough not to deny disorder, the *noise*, the sound and the fury. Clearly, we will have to retain the word *noise*, the sole positive word for describing a state we otherwise can only designate in negative terms, such as disorder. The noisy sea is always there, present, dangerous. To be sure, it's enough to make one shudder with fear. Leibniz lumps everything into the differential, and under the numberless thickness of successive orders of integration. The mechanism is admirable. No one ever went so far in rational mastery, down into the innermost little recesses of the smallest departments. The straight line of reason that must turn its back on this chaos is the ascent into those scalar orders. That way lies before us, it is infinite, the perfect flat projection remains inaccessible. It is divine, it is invisible. (What *noise* does the classical age repress, to what clamor does it close its ears, in order to invent our rationalism?) There, the masterwork is unknown.

The Foot

Balzac saw it, he recognized it. And I can show that he saw it. I can really show that he really knew that he had recognized it: since he signed it with its name. Let me explain.

What then is an ichnography? What then is this masterpiece, where the term "master" does not designate a unique and singular achievement, but rather capital, stock, well—the ichnography? This: the Greek word *ichnos* signifies the imprint of a foot, the trace of a step. As they got nearer, they noticed in a corner of the canvas the tip of a naked foot emerging out of the chaos of colors, shades, faint nuances, a sort of formless fog; but it was an exquisite foot, a living foot! They remained petrified with admiration before this fugitive fragment from an incredible, a slow and progressive destruction. The foot appeared there like the torso of some marble Venus of Paros that might have cropped up amidst the debris of a burned-out city. Here then is the signature by the very name of ichnography. The *belle noiseuse* is the flat projection. Here is the end of our art on earth, says Porbus. From hence, it will be lost in the heavens, says Poussin. Balzac makes us understand that he knows, that he's understood.

The painters have traveled the path Leibniz thought infinite. Breaking down the door, they contemplate the divine floor-plan without understanding. Why don't they?

Because they expected a different painting, one extrapolated, as it were, within the chain of forms. The last, the first of all representations, why would it not still and once again be a representation? Because they were Leibnizians, because they belong to the seventeenth century, because they are classicists.

Ichnography is not harmony, it is *noise* itself. Leibniz's system turns over like an iceberg. This woman before us, stripped at last of her appearances, of her representational trappings, no: she is not the lovely Irene, she is the *belle noiseuse*. She is not harmony, she is racket. She is not peace, she is war. She is not smooth, transparent and blank, she is not one, she is the multiple, and a thundering mix, yes, chaos.

Ichnography is the background noise.

The flat projection was the inaccessible object of metaphysics. It still is. The background noise is this flat projection.

A form of knowledge reputed to be closed is open.

The Possible

The raucous, anarchic, noisy, variegated, tiger-striped, zebra-streaked, jumbled-up, mixed-up multiple, criss-crossed by myriad colors and myriad shades, is possibility itself. It is a set of possible things, it may be *the* set of possible things.

It is not potential, it is the very reverse of power, rather it is capaciousness. This noise is the opening. The Ancients were right to say of chaos that it gaped. The multiple is open, from it is born nature, which is always aborning. We cannot predict what will be born from it. We cannot know what is in it, here or there. No one knows, no one has ever known, no one will ever know how a possible coexists with a possible, and perhaps it coexists through a relationship of possibility. The set is criss-crossed by possible relationships.

Leibniz—him again—constructs this world like an apartment placed at the point, the tip, the apex of a pyramid. Rare, unique, perfect, rigorously calculated within the principles of the optimum, amidst all possible worlds, it stands out like a sheer peak against the mass of shadows. Below, the pyramid widens its base, down deep, infinitely. In the unfathomable thickness of this foundation, in the obscurity of these multiple conditions, the elements of capacity are buried in their own sleep, awaiting their awakening to some degree of culture. This infinite base cannot be defined by lucid and rigorous rationality. It plunges into the background noise, into the cloudy clamor of the confused.

Balzac depicts the vision opposed to divine architecture. The perfect, optimal, living, existent, quasi-divine form—is a foot. It is at the bottom, the base, the minimum of the vortex. The vision is a sort of tornado with a low point, a noise hole at whose bottom is existence. In reversing this vision, time ascends toward the possible and so does space, while one descends toward the existing form.

~

It is the function of the philosopher, the care and passion of the philosopher to protect to the utmost the possible, he tends the possible like a small child, he broods over it like a newborn babe, he is the guardian of the seed. The philosopher is the shepherd who tends the mixed flock of possibles on the highlands, heavy ewes and shuddering bulls, the philosopher is a gardener, he crosses and multiplies varieties, he safeguards the vastness of the old-growth forest, he is on the watch for the inclemency of the elements, a carrier of new seasons of history and of duration, fat cows and lean cows, the philosopher is the shepherd of multiplicities.

The philosopher is no longer right or rational, he protects neither essence nor truth. It is the function of the politician to be right and rational, it is the function of the scientist to be right and rational; there are plenty of functionaries of the truth as it is, without adding more, the philosopher does not wrap himself up in truth as in breastplate or shield, he does not sing nor does he pray to allay nocturnal fears, he wants to let the possibles roam free. Hope is in these margins, and freedom.

The philosopher keeps watch over unforeseeable and fragile conditions, his position is unstable, mobile, suspended, the philosopher seeks to leave ramifications and bifurcations open, in opposition to the confluences that connect them or close them. He goes back up the thalweg a bit, he climbs the chreod, he is going to graze where branches multiply, where freshets are turbulent, where innovation burgeons forth, on the high plains.

The function of the philosopher, the care and the passion of the philosopher, is the negentropic ringing-of-the-changes of the possible.

~

The multiplicity that he tends is not originary. It was so, to be sure, if and when there was a beginning. But so what? The multiplicity of the possible is here, it is now. It is intermediary between the phenomena, it rustles in the midst of the forms that emerge from it. I am quite happy for Proteus to live on an island and for him to tend the marine fauna at sea. When a phenomenon, a form, a relatively durable state, a period, a coherent era, whatever, do appear, they do their best to obscure the extreme fragility of their origins and the absence of their legitimacy. Not everything always has the legitimacy claimed and produced, right and reason are often completely subsequent to foundation. Everything is founded in the possible, all representations originate in the *belle noiseuse,* all states come to us from chaos. The most common forgetting is that of the possible. It is so much forgotten that it is not visible. Even Poussin fails to see this roaring sea, he fails to hear it. There is chaos, there is a circumstance, and suddenly there's the whole foundation. There is the background noise, then a noise in the midst of that background noise, and suddenly there's the whole song. There is the perennial surge, then a fluctuation in that surge, and suddenly there's the river of Time. There is the Roman mob, turbulent, restless, powerful, magnificent, there is the throng and the multitude, there is the population, what chain of little circumstances made it glide all along its history? The crowd is always there vehicle of the possible. The surge is always there carrier of a thousand temporalities, chaos is always present to serve as foundation, noise is always there to invent new musics and new harmonies. The *belle noiseuse* is always present, a cornucopia from which myriad forms emerge, the bottom of a well with pictures of genius. The multiplicity of times escorts our miserable little temporality, the multiple gapes, it is always open. Yet the possible is only there if there are keepers, precisely, only if there are shepherds to tend their flocks on the highlands, only if there are watchers. Philosophy is the vestal of the possible, it is the vestal of time, it maintains the sacred flame during dark hours.

Politics pares down the possible in order to remain stable and maintain sanity; economy, religion, the army, Jupiter, Mars, and Quirinus, and the administration of our day which synthesizes them, have the function and a passion to reduce multiplicities, to reduce possibilities, to work at the confluences. The social functions of power grapple with time. Science is collaborating, when it trims back the bifurcations in order to get nearer its truth. The philosopher is the keeper of multiplicities, he is thus time's shepherd, he seeks to preserve the possibles. And that is why he will no longer find himself either within a function or within a power. For the first time, he is experiencing the separation of philosophy and State. He calls on science, summons it to his side, on the side of knowing, in other words, inventing, not on the side of control. The philosopher lets it be said that the real is rational, for he lets everything be said, including silly things and cruelties, he lets it be said that the rational is the only real. He lets it be said; alas, he lets it be. That the real be rational, that the rational be real, that's what they say, to be sure, but above all, that's what they do, that's what they construct. We construct a real which is a rational one, we construct *a* real, among many possibilities, which is *a* rational one, among other possibilities, just as we pour concrete over the ground. It isn't the only possible concrete, and it is not the only possible covering. City dwellers always think that the constructed world is a landscape, and some country folk believe that the landscape is the world as such. The old rationalism is the concrete of the world, the philosophy of language is the concrete of meaning, our philosophies of politics and history are the concrete of time. There are other possible worlds, I know other possible meanings, we can invent other forms of time. And this is why the philosopher broods over the possible as if it were a fragile newborn babe, like a bouquet of times, like a multibranched candelabrum, like a living network of veins and fibrils, he harkens to the noises and the ringing of changes.

The Apparition of Forms

The *belle noiseuse* is the sea, the nautical murmur.

The flat projection is the noise, the ichnography is the background noise, any scenography, any profile, and any appearance, are forms sprung from this background, signals come from this noise, perceived things born of these apperceptions.

The multiplicity of colors and hues, the turbulent chaos, the maelstrom, a whirling top, is balanced on a foot, on the trace of a foot.

Aphrodite, beautiful goddess, invisible, standing up, is born of this chaotic sea, this nautical chaos, the *noise*. Aphrodite, standing, her foot upon this sea, walks upon this sea. We know only Aphrodite, if that. We turn away from the waves to admire the wave-born.

Mary the Egyptian about to cross the river, and the first Adam of Mabuse the father, and the beautiful woman portrayed in the style of Giorgione, so many beautiful pictures, so many beautiful painted women are born of this beautiful noisy Eve, sea, mother, matrix, fabulous uterus, impregnated by Uranus's brush dripping with spermatic and bloody color.

How is Venus born from the sea, how is time born from the noisy heavens? How are forms born from the formless? How is peace born from the *noise* and the social contract from the restless mob's plundering in every sense and in every direction? How are harmony, singing, sound, rhythm, and song born from this noise?

～

Listen. *Walls, town, and port, death's resort, gray deep where breathes the breeze, all sleep. In the plain is born a noise. It is the breath of the night. It bellows like a soul that a flame forever follows. The higher voice seems a jingle bell. Of a leaping dwarf it is the canter. It dashes, bounds, then in cadence, on one foot . . . dances at the tip of the swell.* Fluctuation.

～

Listen then to another possible voice. Music. *At first, a faint sound, skimming along the ground like a swallow before the storm, whispers and flits* pianissimo, *and sows as it goes the poisonous stroke. Some mouth gathers it up, and* piano, piano *skillfully slips it into your ear. The harm is done, it sprouts, it creeps, it makes its way, and* rinforzando *from mouth to mouth it goes like the devil; then all at once, don't know how, you see Calumny rise up, hissing, swelling, growing right before your eyes; it darts forward, spreads its span, whirlwinds, encircles, wrests, sweeps off, explodes and thunders, and becomes, Heaven be thanked, a* general outcry, *a* public crescendo, *a* universal chorus *of hatred and proscription.* The heinous, hideous *noiseuse.*

2

The Ballet of Alba

FACES AND BODIES
THOUGHTS
MONEY
YOUTH
GYMNASTICS
CALCULATIONS
BARS
NOTES
CORPS DE BALLET
ALBA
TEACHING CORPS
MAGIC
STAR

I begin again.

Two famous painters, Poussin and Porbus, enter the studio of a third painter, their master. He is old, he is a genius, he appears to be demented, perhaps he is imaginary. He has concealed from everyone, and his whole life, his masterpiece, *La Belle Noiseuse*. A veil of green serge masks the canvas.

Poussin and Porbus have come in. They lift the green veil. Before them, the canvas is now nothing but a delirious chaos of colors, shades and forms, a disorder with nothing to be seen or understood in it. In a corner, however, a foot, alive, delightful, beautiful, is left from this destruction.

27

Poussin and Porbus, bent over the canvas, nonplussed, gaze. Behind them, Gillette, the model, naked, silent, forsaken, starts to cry.

Balzac has told, in *The Unknown Masterpiece,* how nakedness stands up in the face of disorder. The unknown is the naked and the multitude of confusion.

Faces and Bodies

We sometimes encounter bodies of such a singular nature, that they do not let convention have their face; their mannerisms belong to no one but themselves. We can recognize them anywhere and at any time, they're so unusual. They are themselves, and they are only themselves, that's what they are, that alone. If these individuals, such oddballs, had nothing banal about them at all, we might deem them a bit more than eccentrics, we might be a bit worried, perhaps we would shuffle them toward the asylum. To the conventional we also owe communication between ourselves. There must be stereotype in every face. No doubt the old painter of the unknown masterpiece was said to be demented for having gone all the way with the singular qualities of the *belle noiseuse.* Right down to the most infinitesimal detail of what changes. Whoever is only oneself is an autist.

This insularity puts a symmetrical generalization in relief. We encounter whores and soldiers and statesmen as well. We seldom examine their faces and their bodies. The women walk by, the men march along, they offer themselves but do not give themselves. Contrary to what the caricaturist or impressionist leads one to suppose, the public man is unrecognizable; he is no longer a particular person. He is now only an operator for mimicry. He erases from his body every angle of singularity, he is moulded of smooth planes. His glance does not pause on anyone, his mask fills in his wrinkles, he softens toward the commonplace any originality. An expressionless public body, invested with conventionality, stereotype, he is a concept, he is a class, he is a quasi-object. Psychiatric asylums shelter super-subjects; political institutions reward infra-subjects. These habitats are symmetrical, as I have already said.

~

One need only bear in mind the one-multiple starred schema for these things, already simple, to become clear. The whore and the statesman have relations only with the multitude. They have to become a common denominator. The makeup girl covers the face to be seen on television with viscous cream, and it is not, as we think, a simple matter of lighting, it is that the public man dons the theatrical mask, which the Latins called persona. You who enter here, erase all difference, leave aside any singularity. Might as well be done with them once and for all, and give your skin that pure capacity for multiplicity. Might as well not be anybody anymore, a pure abstract phantom that every viewer thinks he recognizes. This one who lets himself be seen by the multitude is also in search of ichnography.

Symbol was what the Greeks called a broken, jagged, uneven, fragment of terra cotta, which fitted precisely only the other fragment of the same break. The unique relationship between two singular units reveals specificity in space. An elaborately cut key has the same relationship to the original lock. It has no relationship to other locks. Rub out the crenellations of the key, the crenellations of the symbol, and their stereospecificity is obliterated; the key fits into an increasing number of locks, the symbol adapts to an increasing number of fragments. Made smooth, the key becomes a passkey. The one-multiple relationship gets easier and easier the more indeterminate the one is. If it is determined, it excludes much, it denies, the symbol fits no one, the key is almost of no use. Multiply the notches, and the key becomes autistic, solipsistic. If the one is not determinate, if it is close to nothing or in the neighborhood of no one, it fits in multiple ways. The phantomatic face moves in the direction of the abstract. The more it is smooth and blank, the more customers it attracts in its hollowness. Suetonius said that Caesar was the wife of all husbands and the husband of all wives. Caesar was more of a statesman in this respect than he was in the Gallic wars.

~

Here on this smooth face is the capacity of the multiple that can be called the possible. There is the complex and noisy possible, there is the blank virtual. There is chaos by a superabundance of presence, there is chaos by blank absence. The whore with the ghoulish makeup is woman, a possible woman, the dim and whitish womanizer is a possible man, the statesman, with wan face and bland tone, is a promise of anything; the weathervane takes a direction from the changes of the breeze.

At the limit whoever is capable of anything should be called nobody. Singular reliefs, razed, are submerged by the rising white waters. The whore and the statesman can do anybody. Ulysses king and lover of Circe—the metamorphosis woman—Ulysses's name is nobody. His mask roams at random over the waters. Ulysses is cunning, he adapts. Ulysses is cunning, capable of anything and of anyone, male or female. Ulysses is possible, he is smooth, his name is nobody, he is blank.

He wears a uniform, he has no face, he is blank, Curiatius, a soldier of Alba, advances.

Thoughts

Who am *I*, now that I am thinking? The answer to the question depends on its indetermination. Either I think, or I think something. I think does not mean that I think something. I think means the very activity that thinks, moves, grows and awakens me, which develops like ivy in a place hard to assign that appears to have some collocation in me. Can I think without thinking something? To be sure. But when I think this object, that subject, there is no doubt that I am this subject, that object, if truly I think them; when I think a given concept, I am entirely this concept, when I think tree, I am the tree, when I think river, I am the river, when I think number, I am through and through and from head to toe, number. That is the unquestionable experience of thinking. No invention, no innovation without it. This verb *to be* is also a blank domino, a joker. The hand is no longer a hand when it has taken hold of the hammer, it is the hammer itself, it is no longer a hammer, it flies, transparent, between the hammer and the nail, it disappears and dissolves, my own hand has long since taken flight in writing. The hand and thought, like one's tongue, disappear in their determinations.

When I just plain think, without a direct object complement, without determination, who am I? Who am I, beyond the joy coming from this shudder of awakening, the growth of this green ivy, this dancing flame, this living fire? I think in general, I am a capacity to think something, and I am virtual. I think in general, I can think anything. I think, therefore I am indeterminate. I think, therefore I am anyone. A tree, a river, a number, an ivy, a fire, a reason or you, whatever. Proteus. I think, therefore I am Nobody. The I is nobody in particular, it is not a singularity, it has no contours, it is the blankness of all colors and all nuances, an open and translucent welcome of a multiplicity of thoughts, it is therefore the possible. I am, indeterminately, nobody. If I think. I am nothing and I am nobody. I think, therefore I am not. I think, therefore I do not exist. Who am I? A blank domino, a joker, that can take any value. A pure capacity. There is nothing more abstract. I am just the plain whore of the thoughts that accost me, I wait for them, morning and evening, at the crossroads, under the statue of the angel Hermes, all wind and all weather. And, maybe, I *am*, maybe, if the verb *to be* is a joker or a blank domino, as well.

Would Descartes have said to the clever genie, in his little firegrotto, Ulysses's word to Polyphemus the giant: Nobody? And who is this evil monster, with the single eye and the multiple name? The naked possibility named Nobody enters the lists against the monster multiplicity. Crueler than him, more lucid than the one-eye, he blinds him. Alas! the multiple is always sacrificed.

～

Fluctuating and diverse, he deceives us, Montaigne is more profound than he lets on or than we have let it be said or heard said. His mixed text, who can tell the rationalists' contempt for this mix, goes with *La Belle Noiseuse*, a chaos of forms and hues, a superabundance and a luxury of circumstances, but it goes with absence, blankness, water that ripples and upon which one does not write. Diverse like the multiple, fluctuating like capacity. The sea makes the background noise, but the sea has no memory. Noisy with original singularities, Montaigne is blank, aqueous, and translucent. Michel is all others, the individuals, the ancients, his friend, his other, and Michel is Nobody. This self depicted is the sum of the others and of nothing.

Indetermination is of two kinds: it is either chaotic or blank.

Money

Sometimes one reads pages that are full. So full, so saturated with meaning that they are noisy with it. No one understands the chaotic, no one understands pure singularity. Those pages cannot be exchanged.

One sometimes reads pages that are empty, so light in meaning that they circulate with ease. One has seen and one sees ultimate pages, as if at zero meaning, the pages of money. Blank pages, null and void of meaning, indeterminate, they are pure capacity. Money is the general equivalent, it is worth everything and it is worth itself, money is the joker, it has all values, it has all meanings, having none, smooth as a subject, white as a whore, an abstraction, a politician.

The text nearest money is the one that is blankest.

Money is what one writes when one no longer has anything to write, money is what one sends to people when one no longer has anything to say to them.

Money is indeterminate, it is everything, a kind of general equivalent, it is nothing, a kind of blank meaning.

Information, as blank meaning, is in the process of taking its place, as general equivalent.

Youth

Do not think that youth has fresh skin and a smooth face for simple biochemical reasons. There are reasons for these reasons themselves. Let's have a look. Irreversible time flows down, it flows down from its source to the deltas, from birth toward death. The relation of a human infant to his future forms a kind of fan, his time can flow along multiple beds. The relation of his body to its own future is the same quite abstract relation that the blank subject has to his thoughts, that the nonspecialized hand has to the tools that determine it, that the whore has to her customers, or that money has to the written text. The more the human body is young and the more it is possible, the more it is capable of multiplicity, and the more time it has: not time in its length and duration, but the more kinds of time, the more varieties of river beds it has to flow down, the more valleys it has before it. The more undetermined it is. The old man's interest lies in his determinateness, his body has as a whole become memory, his skin is worn away, like, at the Ganges delta, or the earth or the map. Each somewhat sluggish arm of the delta is encumbered with gravel that can recount the details of upstream. His body is saturated with singularities. The *belle noiseuse* is a naked old lady. The chaos of colors, forms, shades, is perhaps only due to the progressive invasion of space by the monuments of history. The entire volume of the old body is occupied by archives, museums, traces, narratives, as if it had filled up with circumstances. Yes, the old master is mad, he is in the unique and irreversible groove of his singular essence, he has painted his self-portrait. The Ganges has filled up with gravel and sand, messages no longer go through, the channels are saturated with noise, the *belle noiseuse* is drowned in this sound, she is immersed like Achilles in the waters of oblivion, except for her heel, her foot, her fragility. Old age fades away, determined by the rumor of its memory, fixed by the *noise* of its history.

The old madman has painted his self-portrait, like Dorian Gray, the painting is gray like the floor of studios where all hues have fallen. Here, the *noise* is no longer possibility, it is its opposite, it is no longer the fount of time, but its culmination. Nothing will ever come again from the minglings at the lower end of the Ganges, nothing will ever come again from the surplus of history, nothing ever comes from the gray, from the heaping up of memories, nothing has ever come from the horrible heap of books that bring barbarity back in the name of science and enlightenment. Gillette, in back of everybody, a source behind our forgetting, beautiful, naked, white, smooth, bewails the clear origin of the waters. Youth matricial and translucent.

No, no—the newborn babe, shriveled, wrinkled, like an old man, is antique like a book. He is encumbered with the gravel that has come down from phylogenesis, he is the antiquity of the world. The *belle noiseuse* on the other hand is about to be born, she is just being born, she is on the verge of being born. She is nature herself. She barely frees herself from the accumulated libraries of her history. She descends from this chaos with difficulty, she kicks away the learned memory storage with her foot, only the foot of this clamorous kick comes down from this cloud, one must still wait for the delivery, for Aphrodite's natural birth.

When she is born, she will be sixteen, she will be twenty years old, I don't know, I don't recall, she will be Gillette's age, the year zero, white and naked, of beginning.

The old man dies in noise, we die in noise. The *belle noiseuse* is born in *noise,* nascent nature begins in *noise.* Gillette is born in white blankness, nascent nature is born in white blankness. There is the blank white origin. There is the end in noise, as there is the end in blankness, swooning.

The two chaoses are always there, as end and beginning.

Gymnastics

It is imperative to be nothing, all you need to think is to be no-body. The hygiene of thinking, the asceticism of thinking, comes down to gymnastics. Gymnastics means one seeks nakedness. Not that it is a question of taking off one's clothes. One *can* remove one's clothes, that isn't the point. Gymnastic or gymnosophic or gymnopedic nakedness is very close to the absence that thinks. Nakedness goes back to the undetermined. To dismiss every opinion from one's mind, every idea, every hate, is to level off the contours of opinionated determination, it is to find the bare and barren plain. The unwritten wax tablet has lost, forgotten its determinations, with no writing, it is un-differentiated. Opinion is stable, it is stiff, it is singular, it defines someone through hates. The opinionated person is differentiated like a lobster's claw. Inventive thinking is unstable, it is undetermined, it is un-differentiated, it is as little singular in its function as is our hand. The latter can make itself into a pincer, it can be fist and hammer, cupped palm and goblet, tentacle and suction cup, claw and soft touch. Anything. A hand is determined, accordingly. So what is a hand? It is not an organ, it is a faculty, a capacity for doing, for becoming claw or paw, weapon or compendium. It is a naked faculty. A faculty is not special, it is never specific, it is the possibility of doing something in general. To talk about the faculties of the soul is a great misnomer, when we are differentiating between them: the soul is also a naked faculty. It is nakedness. We live by bare hands. Our hands are that nakedness I find in gymnastics, that pure faculty, cleared up by exercise, by the asceticism of un-differentiation. I think, un-differentiated. Thus I am anyone, animal, element, stone or wind, number, you and him, us. Nothing. Nobody. Blank. Bare.

Our body comes down time, it comes down the valley, the thalweg of difference. It runs fatally along determination. Cracking with rheumatism, gnarled, arborescent, daily inured to one gesture and only one, the hand becomes a mere terminal, either technical or bestial. Old Renoir's hand is the organ of the painter species. Difference is our old age. Metamorphosis, metempsychosis, tragic moments when our body altogether collapses into kingdom, phylum, class, order, family, and genus. These aren't fables, or myths, or tall tales, this is the regular and physical march of time toward the determined. The beast difference cries help in the direction of beauty undetermined. *La fontaine*, the fountain of indifference invents fables with stable forms ... The joint loses—as they put it in mechanics—a certain degree of free play, it ends up with only one drift, its difference. The hand becomes a mere clamp, the body a mere animal, and thought becomes a mere opinion. They have lost their freedom.

Gymnastics does not require that one get naked to exercise freely. Quite to the contrary, it freely exercises in order to rediscover nakedness. It is a practice for going back in time. It undifferentiates the body, it seeks to put it into the state of a bare hand. It turns the body into a hand, a subject, a pure faculty. It turns the body into a faculty. It turns it into a capacity. It turns it into a possibility. Gymnastics bleaches the body. There it is, in the abstract.

It has become the naked body of nobody.

I think naked and I am nobody.

I dance naked, I am nothing.

~

Walls, town, and port, death's resort, gray deep where breathes the breeze, all sleep. In the plain is born a noise. It is the breath of the night. It bellows like a soul that a flame forever follows. The higher voice seems a jingle bell. Of a leaping dwarf it is the canter. It dashes, bounds, then in cadence, on one foot dances at the tip of the surge.

The djinn emerges, a dwarf, small, from the plain, from the

night. From the gray deep, the flat plain, the black night, the walls. It dances.

No, this is not the day of the anadyomene Aphrodite, it is the bad night of minor ills.

The djinn dances on one foot. I do not know whether the foot comes out of the silence or the racket. All is sleeping, the plain is a plane, the box is black, zero. It is born amid the noise of the gray deep and the breeze, the background murmur. There is the nought, there is the multiple, and both are possibles. The dance is born out of blankness, bareness, or, on the contrary, out of clamors.

~

The foot looms there, alive and exquisite, dancing, at the crest of a surge, a strange fluctuation midst the fury and the sound of the *belle noiseuse,* drowned in the chaos of multiplicities. Nicolas Poussin and Porbus are bent forward. They are heedless. They do not notice, behind them, naked Gillette. Nude. The original nude and the spring of tears, enveloped in neglect, Botticelli's *Derelitta* at the foot of his wall of paint. The dereliction of nudity, the dereliction of the possible or the dereliction of the origin, the dereliction of freedom. They can no longer think of blank multiplicity. Fools.

Gillette weeps, forsaken, unthinkable, invisible since she is naked. She is the bare faculty, undetermined, undifferentiated, one never scrutinizes anything but differences in the hate and the *noise:* the collapse of time, the collapse of thought roll toward determination. She is naked, she is only possible, she weeps, forsaken, nobody thinks of asking her what *she* sees, of the *belle noiseuse,* whether she sees the picture and what *she* sees, of it, in the light mist of her tears. She sees, she does not tell. She doesn't get lost in meaning, she loves. She begins even to hate a bit, already she is descending the slope of difference, she puts out her foot onto it.

Here is nakedness, there is multiplicity, and they are both possibilities, capacities. Two origins: the river Albula, smooth, naked and white, and the Roman crowd, striated, variegated, zebra-streaked, tiger-striped, the mix. There is silence, there is clamor. The great distinction of multiplicities shifts: there are complex, chaotic multiplicities, sets of a mix at the very extreme of order and disorder, and it scarcely matters whether they are continuous or discrete, there are great white multiplicities. The flat plain on the one hand, and the noise of the gray sea. The dark night when all is sleeping and the breeze breathes and brings a smile to the sea's face. They are not between them contradictory, like the continuous and the discrete, both of them are endings and consummations, both of them are possibilities, sources. Empedocles called them love and hate. Balzac called them Gillette and the *belle noiseuse*. They are not between them contradictory, for the *belle noiseuse* is drowned in the totality of the contrarieties. Love is not the reverse or the opposite of hate, since hate is the whole of contradictions, or the totality of *noise*, sound and fury. The *belle noiseuse* is drowned in noncompossibles. History and knowledge are wholly submerged in the mad painting of *La Belle Noiseuse*. So there is the un-differentiated, flat and bare like the hand, blank like the subject, fragile, suspended, forlorn, on the verge of being born, there is the ocean of *noise*, the surge of differences and determinations.

The *belle noiseuse* and the *belle danseuse*.

Calculations

"A calculator was needed, it was a dancer that got it." Figaro, in the night, makes laughter explode. Thus spoke Beaumarchais. The short-circuit from dance to calculation, of course, blinds this laughter with an intense white light.

Could the dancer's body be like a number? And his nakedness be what is called, in calculus, the unknown quantity? The unknown masterpiece. The unknown quantity can assume all values. It is the possible. Now, the dancer's body can assume, can suddenly take on, all shapes. It is the possible, as well. The dancer and the calculator are in the same blank space. And they encounter money there.

Let us change space and time to get a better look, let us go to Utopia. The king is seeking a prime minister, a sort of finance official, a calculator, an administrator, a treasurer. Or else: the frogs are looking for a king. Everyone has known since Nabussan, son of Nussanab, son of Nabussun, son of Sandusna, that, in order to govern a country, a sublime science designates the very first, the very second economist of the country. The whole question is in the selection. These things require a superior knowledge, inaccessible to those who are only well-read. But since the dawn of times, the selection has missed the mark. Before the arrival of the wise Zadig among us, the greatest of the tax-collectors was always the greatest plunderer. All to himself a whole population for the plundering. Thus speaks Voltaire.

Zadig organizes the choice, the election or the selection. The candidates are sixty-four. They are clad in light silk. There are the candidates, thus clad in the candid and integrity-white gown, all wrapped up in possibility. The candidate, as his name indicates, is white. No one is marked by the future, no one is responsible for it, the candidate is white like the Albula, he is at the beginning of history, within the possibility of political time, he is undetermined. Thus he must be made to dance. He is blank, he is nought, he is without determination, un-differentiated; he is bare, virginal, he can dance. Zadig makes him dance. Zadig is right to make him dance. Zadig is a wise philosopher, and the candidate a phantom.

Before joining in the dance, the candidate goes through a hall where the king's treasures are scattered about, and he must pause there a while. The king's treasures: today we would say the nation's accounts, the gross national product, or the budget, whatever, those things. He stays there a while, I fear it is the calculator's moment. Consider how the candidate dances as he comes out of these lethal minutes of economy. Heavy, lumbering, his head down, arms pinned to his sides, he seems to be encumbered by a certain determination. Weighted down with differences, he is no longer so candid.

A calculator was needed, it was a dancer that got it: covered in silver and gold.

Beaumarchais's idea, a briefer one, is more clear-cut, more true than the little Voltairian utopia. There is of course no question of speaking, even for a half a second, of peculation. Only indetermination is at issue. All the blank whites, all at once, join in the dance.

Whoever dances is cloaked in a candid gown, transparent or white, what difference does it make, he is cloaked in number and gold. He who dances is a numeral and a sign, he is calculation, pure money, his body in the abstract, naked and null, is the general equivalent. Voltaire, with his slight levity, is heavily mistaken. The candid dancer cannot be weighted down by gold. When his head is high, his look assured, his body straight, his leg firm, his arms free, un-differentiation is complete, the dancer is absent, he is as abstract as money and number. Here is a constellation of stars moving from a unique point, absent, toward totality.

Money is bereft of meaning, it has all the meanings. It is blank and polysemous.

Money is pure number and naked calculation. They are faculties. Abstraction.

The dancer is bereft of meaning, he has all meanings. He is blank and polysemous.

The short-circuit is blinding. No, neither money nor calculation can put a stop to the dancing. Each time a dancer *had* to get the spot. Dance is the body of calculation.

Bars

How can one understand such a torture and how tolerate the pain of these dislocations? Why the mercilessness of these bars and this detailed destruction of the body proper? Why this frantic return to the scattered limbs? Does the spectre of death lurk in dance? It took me a long time to forget the press of romance and sex, in order to accede to this nakedness. Memory, however, preserves the hard odors of embrocations and restores the fabulous antiquity of gymnastics. From what mists of time does this absence return to us?

Why this torture? For nothing, literally, for *nothing*. The difficult technique of returning to zero. A path toward nakedness, indetermination, non-existence. The more I think the less I am me. If I think something, I am that something. If I simply think, I am no longer anyone. In any case, me thinking am nothing.

The more I dance, the more I am naked, absent, a calculation and a number. Dance is to the body proper what exercise of thought is to the subject known as I. The more I dance, the less I am me. If I dance something, I am that something or I signify it. When I dance, I am only the blank body of the sign. The sign is a transparency that tends toward its designation. The dancer, like the thinker, is an arrow pointing elsewhere. He shows something else, he makes it exist, he makes an absent world descend into presence. He must thus himself be absent. The body of the dancer is the body of the possible, blank, naked, nonexistent. This dislocation is polysemy come down into the limbs, and these far-flung limbs are an alphabet, a series of scales. The body becomes, at best, undetermined, as un-differentiated as a hand, a digit, a letter, a numeral. The dancer is a semaphore. And semaphore is nothing if it transmits no signal. Have you at times heard language beyond earshot of any specific meaning? Have you heard the noise of thinking, outside individual thoughts? Have you heard naked language, naked thoughts, as faculties?

The semaphore dancer has given himself a faculty-body, a pure possibility of doing. Nakedness here is not the height of concreteness, the complete presence of individual particularities, an unquestionable sign of the proper noun in the body proper, nakedness here is, on the contrary, the height of abstraction, the abstract as such, or the possible here actualized. The individual naked body draws toward its own individuality. It tempts, as they say. The dancer's naked body signifies or evokes, you look at it without seeing it, it makes you see elsewhere. Once again, it is Nobody. It is, literally, broken. A foot knows how to move in every possible direction, a leg, an arm, a hand, a torso, can move in all possible directions. The body is spatially broken in every sense and direction. It becomes, then, capable of every meaning, every sign, every designation.

The body has become the joker, the substance, the cat's-paw, the prop of all possible meanings. It can say everything without language. The body's articulations are broken in order to flee articulate language.

All come to dance in order to read without speaking, to understand without language. They are all, nowadays, so exhausted, so saturated, so hagridden with discourse, language, writing. In the end fugitive meaning passes through there, taciturn.

The dancer's body is the Platonic *chôra*, the virgin wax on which one writes, pure location or pure place or naked space.

Who am I when I am thinking? A naked space. Who am I, dancing body? A naked space. Unprotected by any rampart of singularities.

Without the aid of qualities. The body without qualities.
The reverse of the painting of the *belle noiseuse*.
Gillette naked.

Notes

One can dance only to music. Music transports the universal before meaning. Music has only a blank meaning. It is the universal language, nearly undetermined.

Music is an un-differentiated language.

The body of indifference bathes in undetermined sonority.

The rhythm beats, reversible, the struggle against irreversible time.

Music plays just shy of any singular meaning.

The dancer moves his sign-body, in the space occupied by signals before the sign.

Corps de Ballet

I am not taking a census, I do not have the means to make a complete review, I am not doing an inventory, I am calling forth, conjuring up with my hand the undetermined places, things, beings that are un-differentiated.

I summon them in a place.

First, the whore comes forward, because she's the one who leads the dance. She is seated at the crossroads, where points come in and whence they depart, she dances in the star's place, she is wearing a peacock tail. She is seen by a hundred eyes, she sees a hundred lookers-on. She dances a pas de deux with the candidate, wearing that blank probity, she dances a pas de deux with the statesman, white ghosts of polyvalences, with the soldiers.

I summon the ballet, I call forth in this place the corps de ballet.

It is a matter of a ballet, indeed, it is a matter of a ballet in white, perhaps it is the ballet of all ballets.

Crafty Ulysses swarms all over the place, worms around. He flutters about, blankly, he is transparent. He dances a pas de deux with the monster Polyphemus. His name is Nobody, he is polysemous, for he has several meanings, all meanings, several names, all names, for he does several steps, all steps, several signs, all signs. He has several eyes, all eyes, in front of the monster with a single eye, he has a thousand eyes like the peacock tail, ocellate. He is Nobody, he is any number of bodies. Polyphemus has only one eye, yet he has a name of multiplicity. The blank dances with the multiple, and the multiple dances with the one. Each takes a place and gives up his place. The subject without character, the subject without quality, fragile, trembling, suspended, proliferates, vanishes, flickers at the edge of existence. A space where each gives up his place to all, a sum space of all places given up. The *noise* is the sum space of the places taken.

Caesar the wife dances with a number of husbands, Caesar the husband dances with a number of wives.

I call forth the absences, the nudities, the blank pages, the matrices. I summon the phantoms which fade away the further they come forward. I call forth the court of the un-differentiated.

The court of the king, Caesar, the statesman, premier star dancer in the company of the whore, dragging that peacock tail.

I imagine a ballet which would be the dancer's body. A ballet naked and undetermined like his supple hand, a ballet un-differentiated like his nimble leg, his foot naked in the noisy sea, a ballet indifferent and naked as the body of young Gillette. The king is the dancer's hand, the whore is the dancer's foot, and the calculator is the body, the torso of the dancer.

The ballet absents itself as the dancer's body absents itself, limbs with freedom to the hundredth degree, as the unknown quantity of the calculator abstracts itself, a sign with hundreds and with thousands of values. An abstract ballet of abstract bodies, a sign ballet of the sign's bodies.

A ballet covered in gold and silver, a ballet void of sense before any meaning, the dancers, the whore and the statesman, who decidedly never let go, exchange amongst themselves smooth symbols, signs transparent as passkeys, gold and silver.

Entrance exit of the calculator, entrance exit of the mathematician, entrance exit of the thief, the banker, the retailer, the treasurer, entrance exit of the god Hermes, bearer of the closed letter, the purloined letter, the letter void of meaning before any meaning, money.

Ballet of absences and ballets of transference, I call forth, absent, a ballet of abstractions. They are abstract because they have found nakedness.

The Greeks invented the abstract through having dared to strip naked the gods.

Entrance of the gymnast in gymnopedy, entrance of the gymnosophists, entrance of the professor of gymnastics.

They teach the king, the kings, how to come to be naked, they teach the candidates the sloughing of the white gown, they teach the whores, the calculators, the mathematicians, the paunchy financiers to take off their heavy multiplicities, to forget, for once, their quarrels, their *noises*. Take off the meaning, and you will dance.

When the sign loses its meaning, when it loses all possible meanings, then it becomes pure sign, naked sign, abstract sign, it enters deeper still into calculation, into mathematics, into money, the god is more god than the god himself. The thing becomes a number, the number becomes a letter, the letter itself is a symbol, the information, the software un-differentiates itself, as if it were slowly entering its own faculty, its own nakedness. The professor of gymnastics is the ballet master, he is the master of the gods, of the abstract, he is the professor of blankness.

The Greeks invented numbers and geometry through having had the bizarre notion of this nakedness.

Thus the dancer who is the ballet by himself alone is the most abstract of men . . . All disperse before him, all make way for him, he dances.

He does not dance alone, even if he is dancing alone. Blank, absent, on the brink of nonexistence, he dances with another absence.

Filling all space while the dancer is forever giving up his place, music, crazed, makes him dance, him, the naked sign, it is the universal language. Harmony dismembers him and rhythm makes him flow.

All meaning has vanished from the place that I call forth. It is an entirely blank place. Music transports the universal before all meaning, the body of the dancer carries the universal of the sign before all meaning. On this spot, where the quest pushes us into the center of a fascicle, as into the focal point of fascination, the blank ballet of the transcendental takes place. It says nothing but pure possibility, it says nothing but naked capacity, it is the ballet of the conditional.

The conditions of possibility run, at times, through space, run, at times, through society, they pass through the body of silence, they pass through beauty.

Alba

It is the final ballet. It has no scenario, it has no history. It is the blank ballet, it tells of the climb back up toward Alba. The place I am evoking, the royal place, a crossroads where Caesar passed, the space of the calculator or the dancer's stage, is the place of Alba. Alba is our origin, it is our matrix, under the foundations of the city, it is the mother city. It is, white, the mother city beneath the holy city. It is the place of our birth, its name is Alba the White.

To be worthy of thinking, to know how to calculate, to compose music or a prayer or a poem, to be vested with language, to be worthy of dancing, one must have made one's pilgrimage to Alba the White.

When Zola, in the *Dream*, returns to a completely blank book, where proper names are lost, where the traces of bodies are erased, where the marks of sins are effaced beneath the immaculate cotton, under the chrism of extreme unction, when Melville, across the seven seas, chases the white whale to the death, white with fright, white with ecstasy, when the whaler dies from meeting up with it; when Musil constructs a space and a being without qualities, when I call forth the ballet of Alba, we are all in search of what Plato named the *chôra*, a smooth and blank space prior to the sign: it is the dancer's body and it is the blank page, the virginal wax, where the choreographer writes.

All he ever writes is a variety of this ballet of Alba.

Teaching Corps

I am now only the hand that calls forth. I am the one who recognizes in the dancer his brother, his fellow, myself. He reduced himself to being nothing anymore to show what all is possible, all temporal possibility through rhythm, all possible absence and presence in space. Thus the thinker is nobody in order to become only an attention to every novelty, in order only to be an attention and to attend every unexpected arrival. Whoever thinks is naked and whoever dances is nobody. Both are shy of meaning, both are shy of language, in the neighborhood of noise and music. I bear witness that there is clamor of thought. Whoever thinks never draws attention to himself, whoever dances does not attract people's glances to himself. They summon. Maybe they plead. Likewise, whoever teaches does not bring back around to himself the listening thoughts. What would the teaching body be if it got itself noticed? It would be mere exhibition, a stupid and silly presentation of such common singularities. The teaching corps, like the dancing corps and the thinking subject, is forever evoking, forever invoking, calling, another focus than itself. So naked, so blank, so empty, so absent that it brings forth a presence. Cloaked in candid probity and white gown. Cloaked in a frock coat, or white alb. If at the end of the dance or the lecture, if at the end of attentive and fervent thought, a person previously absent has not now—Hosanna!—unexpectedly arrived, in the latter case, to be precise, philosophy, in the former, to be precise, god or beauty itself, and in any event, perhaps, *us,* if this real ghost has not passed through the door of the theater or the amphitheater, then the dancing corps or the teaching corps have failed in their sign exercise. What do you think the mathematician is doing with his white chalk, on the blackboard? He calls down an absent presence. He makes nonexistent idealities visible, makes them exist. Literally, he makes us believe in them. And that is why his science bears the name of instruction. Here the body effaces itself in order to call forth another body, here the body is annihilated and becomes a tiny pile of ashes in order that the existence of other bodies may rise up, the immense legion of angels of absence.

Yes, the dancer is an archangel. He commands angels, he begins their manifestation.

Magic

There is magic, even there. Yes, I admit it, magic. Don't worry, it is only white magic. The mages dance, the mages signify, the mages calculate, they instruct. Whores, politicians, thinkers, mathematicians.

~

The dancer, in amongst the corps de ballet of Alba, is nonetheless the only hero. A calculator was needed, and the calculator entered the dance. A financier was needed, a king was needed, a musician was needed, they all made their entrance, I even thought for a moment that music here was either first or last. Yes, when the dancer dances alone, he still and always dances with music. Is music ineliminable, in this pas de deux, solitary in appearance?

The dancer is the sole hero, he remains when the others have gone, when music withdraws from the space. He is the sole hero, for he is helpless. His body is helpless, his gestures and the sign that he attempts are not aided. Dance is without recourse. It is alone, and it is first.

The other bodies all have prostheses, even in blank space. This one is covered in cream, that one is covered in money, this one is covered in language, that one is covered in meaning, they all have an object, they all have a support, a cane, a stick—a memory—an image—a sort of faculty, a stick of chalk, a board, a sheet of paper, a stock. Some writing, at least. Gold, symbol, written page. The dancing body is naked, truly, no tricks, naked, nothing in the hand and no sleeve, the dove.

The dancer is the most naked of men and the blankest among the Alba dancers. He is totally abstract, without existence and without recourse.

His body, always, cries out for help.

Dance is a cry for help that never marks itself.

The others have gold, they have a language, they have a sound, they have, outside of their bodies, something their bodies lean upon, however tenuous, even immaterial, the thing may be. They have a written memory in a given spot.

The dancer has nothing, he is nothing.

He is first, he is last.

Star

On the noisy canvas of the mad old man of genius, Balzac shows us the print of a foot. A mark on the canvas, it is not a dance mark, for dance has no memory, nowhere is it printed. The dancer comes forward. She has no feet. She prints no trace upon the space. She is nothing, not even an abandoned memory. She raises her foot, now she's on a point, light, absent, nonexistent. She leaves nothing on the page of my writing. The point is a white stylus, a blank style.

~

Whoever is nothing, whoever has nothing, passes and steps aside. From a bit of force, from any force, from any thing, from any decision, from any determination, the dancer, the dance step aside. The step is a step aside. Thus is movement born, thus is grace born. Grace is nothing, it is nothing but stepping aside.

Thus is movement born, thus, perhaps, is born time.

Not to touch the ground with one's force, not to leave any trace of one's weight, to leave no mark, to leave nothing, to yield, to step aside.

The dancer steps aside. Dance leaves the spot, it gives way to any other. Dance is Alba itself, it is its blank place. To dance is only to step aside and make room, to think is only to step aside and make room, give up one's place.

To leave at last the page blank.

~

I believe that man is blank and un-differentiated. Man has no instinct, man is not determined, man is free, man is possible. Free as a hand, quick as thought, possible as youth, free as dance forms him and breaks him. Free, perverse, insane and rational, capable of anything. And man is nothing. He is naked.

I believe that one can still think of man, universally. But this universal is empty and blank. A universal perverse, man is without attribute. God who had all of them took them all away from him, in the garden between two seas.

God who had all of them gave them all, one by one, to the world, to the plants, to the animals. At the very end of his work, he had nothing left in his hands. He molded man out of this nothing, plain water and soft loam. Man is this last nothing trying to imitate the other creatures.

Upon emerging from the blaze of his hypothetical author, Adam, blank, starts to dance. On coming out of the confinement within her supralapsarian lover, Eve dances with Adam. Man the dancer and the blank white dancer-woman are our first parents.

This is their fault, a fault is a lack, they lack everything. And we still lack any determination.

Then they left, so we leave the page blank.

~

I know what Being is all about.

Being is blank and transparent, quite simply.

Being as Being is blank, so is Being as Word.

~

Blank, undetermined—POSITIVE.

~

Laughter is that little noise, uttered in blank ecstasy.

3

Collective Furor

I retrace my steps.

The trace of a foot on *La Belle Noiseuse* marks an ichnography. From whatever side you look at the painting, you will see only noise in it, you will hear only fury in it. The law of *noise* has no exceptions, whoever turns back violence uses violence. It is in the negative that determination has its infinity.

Feet

Think back to Hercules and Cacus, the old Greek myth revived at the dawning of Rome, think about their herd. Who stole those bulls? Cacus, to be sure, stole those of Hercules, Hercules, to be sure, took them from Geryon, and by what right was this Geryon in possession of them? And who hid them? Cacus hid them in his

49

cave, Hercules had hidden them from view beyond the river, which he crossed by swimming and pushing the herd before him. Cacus reversed the tracks in front of his cave, Hercules, sharper, had obliterated them in the water. Water leaves no traces. If *La Belle Noiseuse* is nautical, if the *noise* is sea noise, the foot printed there cannot there remain. It fluctuates, it does not remain. Or if it remains, it does so by fluctuating. It is one, it isn't one, unstable. Again, who killed whom? Hercules to be sure killed Cacus, but the nearby shepherds were going to settle Hercules's hash. Who is telling the truth, who is lying in this story? The one who says that Hercules is a god? that he is a murderer? that he is, a minute later, a victim? I listen to this story, and I can hear that all the places in it are occupied, almost at one and the same time, by all the characters in the story. Each one in it is guilty, each one is innocent, each one is a victim, an assassin, evil, good, truthful and lying, and so on and so forth. But look closely at the tracks of the bulls' hooves, in front of the cave of the thief, look, until you can look no further, at the hoof marks wiped away on the river. As in the case of *La Belle Noiseuse,* they mark a precisely ichnographic composition. The Greek myth reveals, by hiding it, the totality of the possible. Hercules is a thief, he is a murderer, he is just, he is an ordinary shepherd, he is a god, Hercules is virtual. The space of the narrative is the sum of the places, either taken or given up.

Leibniz was fond of paintings that, from one angle, show a nude woman, from another a scene from history, from elsewhere still a seascape. They are composed on purpose to say everything, under the assumption that from every site their scenography changes. Such is the text of Cacus, a free text, unconstrained, as it is said of a system that it has the whole range of freedom. We are back to Alba the White, and Cacus is bleached blank.

La Belle Noiseuse is a matter of sound, fury. The myth of Cacus is a story of death, fury. Is it necessary that in every trace, that in every ichnographic attempt, fury remains, invariant?

~

Horace is about to die, killed by the Curiatii, killed by his twin, or beneath the blows of that whole crowd that surrounds him. A coward, running away. A courageous man, retracing his steps. A murderer to be killing his wounded enemy thus. The killer of his sister. A conqueror in the end, a victim as well. Praised, condemned, by the people and by the king's tribunal. A national hero, a despicable accused man, an entirely ordinary soldier. A man—in the sense in which I said a blank white man. No, I am not going to retell Horace's story, I'm only showing you the traces of his steps. Which way have they turned? Two ways, all ways. Each time that there is a trace of steps, pay attention to the flat projection. Here we have the lovely foot of the *belle noiseuse,* here we have the marks of the bulls' hooves, here we have the hero who goes back over his own steps. It is quite likely that Horace's story sketches once again the totality of the possible, those warriors are virtualities.

At the beginning of the history of Rome, at the beginnings of our history itself, at the beginnings of our science of history, Livy, in recounting the myth of Cacus or the story of the Curiatii, sets up and puts together a machinery full of wonders. Myth as much as history poses all the questions and gives all the answers, so that they define a curious object, differently viewable from every site. The flat projection machine expresses objectivity, it makes theories manifest, it situates the observers.

What is objectivity? The essence of the object. Don't cavil at the definition, it is a tautology. Now, scenography depends on a point of view, it marks the presence of a subject, it has to do with the observer, with his situation, with his station, with his angle. The object itself encircles its flat projection. Objectivity is ichnographic. The subject has disappeared.

An admirable historian it is that first constructs an ichnography, fabulous is the savant who first defines his object, his objectivity. How can we instead have despised these fables, these myths, these tragic stories? These blank completudes?

From them everything follows. A history trickles down from them as from a spring. Have you noticed that above a spring one inevitably flounders in a swamp or soggy ground? Before the point or the sense is decided, there is a space where all senses are in flux. It is the ichnography of the springs. From this space everything follows. You can always make some history, as I already said. The story can be told, of any object. This, previously unnoticed, is not without consequences. From history told, you can tell everything. All narratives have value, all theories as well. Every site delivers its coherence, invisible from any neighboring site. This, on the contrary, *has* been noticed. What concerns scenographies is always, and banally so, well observed. But what can be said of the genius that goes back to the ichnographies?

Balzac led us toward *La Belle Noiseuse.* She is a thing of nature perhaps, in the midst of the noise of the sea. The *noise* there is the noise of murmur and clamor above all. These myths lead us to the *noise* again, that of history, which is a sound of fury. But I am not sure that it is necessary to rush to separate sound from fury. Let us go on using the word *noise,* nature and history tangential.

But first, why is it that one can compose a flat projection or an object only in sound and fury?

Let's talk about fury.

Fury

The fury of Cuchulain, the little Irishman, back from the battle, and plunged by the women into the cauldrons of water, Horace's fury before and after the fight, the Corneillean fury of Camille's curses, the state of *furor* analyzed by Georges Dumézil, now that's what can be called *noise. Noise* is both battle and racket. The hero marks space with the corpses left by his butchery, he occupies space with his clamors. Camille understood the lesson, she speaks her curses. *She* is the *belle noiseuse.* Horace holds the space where the Curiatii are dying, Rome occupies the blank space of Alba the White, Horace came back by retracing his steps, I guess his cries of rage held the space of the fight, Corneille made us hear them before the battle began. Camille does not want Horace to take up the whole place. She fights, in her way. She howls, rages, and flies into a fury herself. The cause and goal of a squabble are the taking of a place, and noise occupies space. The whole point is to hold, occupy or take a place. Camille attempts to retake the space occupied by Horace's murders. *Noise* against *noise.* Noise against weapon. Noise is a weapon that, at times, dispenses with weapons. To take up space, to take the place, that is the whole point. Rome has just conquered the blank white place of Alba, and so, virtually, universal space, Camille invokes, evokes the universe to bring Rome back to the absence of place. And noise occupies space faster than weapons can. Words and cries are quicker than winged arrows, or Horace's footrace. We are sufficiently aware of this today having constructed the universal of noise.

Horace kills Camille behind the curtain, Camille has failed, she will not hold the space of the stage, held by words nevertheless. There are places held by arms, there are places held by cries and whispers. Every space is thus taken up by *noise*. By fighting or by sound. Horace forces respect for the place of the parade ground, the king will make him respect the place of pleading.

La Belle Noiseuse is in fact, quite simply, an occupied place, the space of the painting, it is a place taken, a place where someone has set a foot down. The print of this foot means that *noise* holds this space, that it has set itself up there. In Greek, they call it: a thesis.

Thesis and Place

Thesis is the action of putting something in a place. What is important is the place, and only then the manner of occupying it. Of taking it, holding it, setting oneself up there. Setting one's foot on it. The foot, here, is the trace of a thesis, and the wall of colors, the *noise*, is at once battle and racket, the two strategies—material and logical, hardware and software—of taking place and getting a foot in the door. Balzac's painting was an unknown masterpiece of philosophy. The antithesis immediately begins the battle, it is contemporaneous with the thesis, the *noise* is henceforth installed, stable, on the spot. I mean: on the board, on the canvas. And I had said: on the boards, on the stage. It has been said: in history.

~

The fury of Camille and Horace, the fury of the little drenched Irishman, are said to be isolated outbursts of a man, or of a woman. A unique, exceptional hero, offered as a blazon for our mimicry. Now, to fly into a fury, one needs enemies, allies, a spectacle of terror. It is necessary to mount, for the warrior, a theater of operations. What would courage be without a display? Matamore[1] is, as far as I can tell, a fine name, which El Cid might have been worthy of. Who prides himself on having cut up some Moor?

Fifes and drums, trumps and oliphants, the military tune leads the march, and everyone knows that the most daring soldiers go no faster than the music. The *noise,* first. Fury is not a solitary matter; when it is, a single person carries on his head, bristling with snakes, the collective passion. Fury belongs too, and above all to the multitude, and the multitude rushes around, it covers space like a flood. The population ravages the place. I will be coming to the throng in fury. It is to forget the press of the throng in fury, to repress the multitude and the population, that the furious hero and the orderly army are made ready, constructed, represented. Corneille saw collective fury better than his model and his critics. He clearly sees that the king orders sacrifices and combats in order to calm the ire of the people. Georges Dumézil is right, one must start with the fury, one must, truly, start with the *noise,* battle and racket, but one must, furthermore, start from the fury of multiplicities.

Background noise is the first object of metaphysics, the *noise* of the crowd is the first object of anthropology. The background noise made by the crowd is the first object of history. Before language, before even the word, the noise.

~

One can go see the ancient gods die at the theater. Where I come from, which hardly exists any more, the sons of country folk, including myself, orphaned forever from their cultural life, go to rugby matches, as if they got life from these games a bit. They live there, every Sunday, the origin of tragedy. Without a script, naturally; without knowing it, fortunately.

Sporting events are not entirely what we think. They are a matter of culture, of one of our ultimate ways of being together. Are you aware of public meetings where the fervor, the faith, the participation are such that they can kill you? Attending some of these meets, I have known of up to three deaths from cardiac arrest. The emotion. How many deaths through emotion are there in political, religious, cultural assemblies these days? The Greeks gagged at a tragedy, mothers gave birth at them from being moved. Contrary to what you see, there is no audience at a rugby match, there is no distance between the group and its team, as there is between the members of an acting troupe and the pit, for example. I'm from here because of my home team, not because of things like my parish, my church, my village, which for their part have disappeared, but in the same way that an Indian might be a fox, a snake or a bison. This is my totem, me and my group together. The ethnologists would do well to give an ear to this, as well as the historians of very primitive religions. The traces of the most deeply buried archaisms are not in the places we think, they are here, in front of us and in us, terrifically live. So powerful that one should watch out for them. Don't look only in books for the origins of rugby, don't just rummage through texts on ancient recreations like the *soule* or the *barrette*, listen to what is shouted in the clamor of the stadium. The secret lies in that noise. That chaos-noise is primitive, like the wind of violence, unleashed, mastered, lost, retaken, delirious, and disciplined. It subsides and swells like action, but it is noise like action: disorder and danger to be controlled. We are an inch away from murder, remember that there have been various deaths there, the gentlemen in question behave, so they say, like hooligans, no, these unleashed hooligans are in a very real sense gentlemen. Just try to lay yourself open to the limits of violence and to behave with dignity. To say that the experience, the regulation that ensues, are cultural, means nothing, it is the source of culture. Just listen to these cries: they are the echo or the encore of the most deeply buried of archaisms. This ceremony is a religious one, by religion I mean the things forever forgotten, barbaric, wild things, for which we have lost the words and which come to us from far, far away, without a text. From bodies to the collective, in a lightning short-circuit, without language, through the groundswell of violence and pandemonium.

Forest, Surge

Macbeth is not alone, in the palace, in the last hours before his death. Every enemy is cutting a branch, in Birnam wood. The forest is moving, it is coming forward, the forest of Birnam is rising on Dunsinane Castle. Space is invaded by this swelling. The forest occupies the empty place, it begins to move. Behind each tree branch is a threat. What is this monster sprung from the surge in Theramenes's narrative? Shakespeare saw and shows what Racine sees and hides. Behind each wave, there was also a man. Shakespeare sees, Racine sees, Corneille saw. Behind Camille's rage the unbound crowd of Rome's enemies floods over the walls. Macbeth's forest, the sea, the seaside, at Hippolytus's death, the deluge of fire, at Camille's imprecations, they are crowds in a furor. Fury is, to begin with, multiple. When the hero is alone, it is because he takes fury upon himself.

The forest is multiplicity. The sea, again, is multiplicity. The increasing deluge, fire, multiplicity always returns. Forest, sea, fire, deluge, figures of the crowd. From the crowd comes fury. The hero in a rage is the one of this multiple. The Greek word that is the origin of this fury means to sacrifice. The hero in a rage is on the sacrificial altar, he is on the stage, on the boards, in front of the crowd of multiplicity.

Macbeth: What is that noise? What then is that *noise?* It is the cry of women, my good lord. The forest of women blows, moans, advances, and threatens. There are, at our backs, cries of the bacchantes. And then Macbeth: Wherefore was that cry? No, it is no longer *noise,* it is a cry. What is this cry, singular, in the midst of the *noise?* What is this signal and why does it stick out in the hubbub? What is this fluctuation in the surge? And what is this jostle midst the chaos, this jolt, this swerve? *Wherefore* this swerve? The queen, my lord, is dead. Dead amongst the women. Amongst the bacchantes?

Macbeth, who can no longer feel terror, bends forward and thinks. He looks closely at the painting. Life, he says, is but a walking shadow, a poor player, that struts and frets his hour upon the stage, and then is heard no more...a tale told by an idiot, full of sound and fury, signifying nothing. In Macbeth's mouth the word *fury* is the final word, the word *noise* was the first. Macbeth, like Poussin, looks closely at the picture, he is convinced that it signifies nothing. What is underneath? Shakespeare is on the same line as Balzac. The *noise* is on the canvas, the *noise* is on the stage. The shadow passes, it is only an appearance. The entire knowledge of appearance is called phenomenology. The sound and the fury, the clinking of arms and the words in the marketplace, are only in the signs whose meaning we do not know. *Noise* occupies the place: painting, theater, appearance, representation. The player is an idiot and the old painter is insane.

~

Caution: even calumny signifies nothing, its collective dynamic is independent of meaning. Here it is.

Dovetail

That soft sound that moves and starts up is like a swallow. A harbinger of spring, a harbinger of the storm, it skims over the ground with its dovetail, it shows the bifurcation. It is the instauratrix, instauration is a Greek word meaning fork, meaning bifurcation, which sketches a cross or a dovetail. In the beginning is the crossroads. The murmur is nothing, is practically nothing, the murmur selects.

It is nought or it increases. Like the noise of a crowd that thunders and rumbles, at times breaks up, and at times gets bigger. At each crossroads, it breaks up or grows further. Noise is parasitical, like interference, it follows the logic of the parasite, a very tiny thing, an insufficient reason, a cause without consequence at times, which may vanish to the left of the dovetail, which may increase and magnify to the right of the instauration. This soft sound which has just begun, which is now impinging on our ears, we have forgotten that it might well have died. It never stops being unstable, left or right, immense or nonexistent, new music or silence.

This interference, this parasite, passes and dies. It passes and nothing takes place. It increases, multiplies, occupies space, there is only it. The work of the parasite changes systems, it mithridatizes them, vaccinates them, changes noise into music, or else the work of this parasitic interference is nought. Skims along the ground, soars, goes from dovetail to dovetail.

Noise sows the poisonous stroke as it goes. As it goes: you will never again see the carrier, the factor. Even the opportunity is erased, the vector vanishes. The cause passes, the effect remains. Let us call this the Hermes effect: we only see the angel passing by if he carries nothing, silence, "an angel is passing," [as is said in French when there is a hiatus]. At the first letter, you see only the letter, Hermes is already far away. The parasitic logic follows a vectorial space, a space through which pass vectors that do not remain.

Noise is the vector, noise is the feathered arrow, noise sows the poisonous stroke as it goes. Parasite logic never stops. The seed-corn dies, and it dies. The seed-corn dies, and it sprouts. It sprouts and it is meager, it fructifies only slightly. It sprouts and it multiplies, exponentially, it overruns the place, it occupies space. Bifurcation is the law, a fork or a dovetail, a feathered arrow, a vector.

Noise sows the poisonous stroke as it goes. The poison is taken, and it passes. The poison is taken, and it remains. It remains, and it cures you. The poison is taken, remains, and it kills. The parasite propagates itself, left or right, finite or nought, poison or remedy, leaping, buoyant, from dovetail to dovetail. The swallow is already far away. I am sure that it was an entire flock of swallows, one swallow doesn't make a spring. But be advised: a single one among them, light, fluctuating, can make a storm or the good old summertime. Noise, stroke, seed-corn, poison, propagation. Space is overrun by bifurcations, by an immense tree.

The word *murmur* in our languages is used to describe a repetitive and straightforward propagation. Likewise for the word *imitation.* The rumor spreading by word of mouth, from one mouth to another, without making a move, always the same: that doesn't exist, or it may happen, once in a while. No, a rumor does not fly along, stable and constant, it rushes forth. It is only a murmur when its voice is hardly audible, at the beginning. No, a rumor goes like the devil. The devil, in Greek, is calumny itself.

A rumor acquires strength at the bifurcations, at each crossing of its forking path. It is willing to die away, it rebounds, rings out in not dying away.

If it were constant and stable, like an imitative murmur, a quasi-object exchanged within the group, and which itself does not change, it would die, in a few short steps, of redundancy. A murmur is redundant, so is mimicry. Papa, mama, immovable families. Bromides. Methodology, a straight path, is, in general, redundant. Rules, criteria, insurances, dying knowledge. Redundancy is needed, of course, for the maintenance of groups and the establishment of institutions, but rumor is not that. Oh yes, it goes like the devil.

Noise is both a vector and a parasite, an opportunity that is erased and a tiny little cause, which, making its way through the intersections, tries its luck at living, heads to the left, tails to the right, yes, a noise goes around choosing to get bigger or die. (In other words, and by way of parallel: if you wish to save your soul, your breath, your voice, venture to lose them; if you wish to lose them, try to save them, to keep them in the cocoon of redundancy.) From the sometimes brief, sometimes middling, and sometimes very long series of those chances, a path is delineated, not a thread, a path so intricate and subtle that the person who could determine its meanderings would be very clever indeed. The path of *noise* is a meandering.

Quite unpredictable and yet predictable. The path occupies space, no one knows where it goes. Intricate, unpredictable, and thus saturated with information, new. Invading the place by successive arborescences, it is predictable, known, redundant. An immense dovetail for a finish: orderly as a chorus, yet out of order, since one does not know what is cried and against whom.

We have never known what a general will was, we have never known its subject, never known its intentions, truly. But we have often heard its chorus. It is the final chord of this meandering in the multiple.

The best word used by Beaumarchais in that description, which will be considered scientific, of the successive bifurcations of a propagation, is the word *whirlwind*. Calumny, he says, whirls like a vortex, it wheels, encircles, wrests up, spreads its span, and magnifies in bursting, explodes. Noise is a turbulence, it is order and disorder at the same time, order revolving on itself through repetition and redundancy, disorder through chance occurrences, through the drawing of lots at the crossroads, and through the global meandering, unpredictable and crazy. An arborescent and turbulent rumor.

~

Space is invaded by an immense arborescence, from dovetail to dovetail, roots, rootlets, trunk, branches, and boughs. The noise runs on, flies, goes from knot to knot, branching unpredictably. These fickle multiple swallows compose a tree, movable and fluctuating, here a demi-cone, a demi-vortex.

Are there other means of invading space or holding a place?

A Gaul shouts on the hill in sixteen directions. Every Gaul who hears, passes on the voice through all the eyes of the winds. At first it is a faint sound; all of Gaul, by the setting of the sun, is up in arms. Or else Gaul heard nothing. Or maybe Gaul, a month later, is still trying to come to an agreement. It depends.

~

In the middle of the demi-cone or at the center of the vortex, lies the object of hate, the subject of proscription. Multiplicity shoves its *noise* onto the one. It crystallizes the *noise*. No longer a multiplicity, no longer noisy, it is one, globally, it is a single chorus, it is one locally, the center, the midpoint, the navel of the vortex: the eye. The eye of the storm. No one has ever seen a chorus being formed except from there. I see, I see the open skies.

Thus have we gone from the soft sound or the quasi-nonexistent cause to the concept, to the universal.

~

An ancient and enduring philosophical tradition says that colors cannot be seen without space, that space cannot be seen without color. Only utopias could be colorless. Color then is the invariant aspect of space, space is the invariant aspect of color. It is a reciprocal proposition. The tradition comes to us from the Pythagoreans and from so far back that at the dawn of geometry a certain variety of space was called color. The Classics, the Moderns, the Contemporaries have reiterated this obviousness. An obviousness that remains ignorant of the multiplicity of spaces, that is a tautology where visual space is concerned. Because no one has ever, to my knowledge, brought up the question of the observer. There must exist some kind of space, or several, for a blind species, the mole in its network of holes, and if, tomorrow, my eyes enter the darkness forever, some space will remain for me, obviously.

While I can close my eyes, at my leisure, while I can cloak my colors, I can neither close nor permanently plug my ears. No one is deaf, in a strict sense; at least intropathetic noise is perceived nonstop, my body burns enough to give it off at all times. Hearing is an open receiver which does not go to sleep. It stays awake along with the tactile sense, the skin and the sense of smell. My sleep leaves vigilant guards, when my sight is cloaked. The parasites, the interference pass through. When the sense of sight is the model of knowing, I am not always thinking. If hearing is the model, I am always thinking. Well, I am always thinking. Hearing, no doubt, is a better model, where the occultations are never total, and where the flashes, at all times, overlap.

The second reciprocal assertion is not stated by tradition. There is no space without noise, as there is no noise without space. One is an invariant aspect of the other, and reciprocally. Background noise is the background of the world, and the world began, it is said, with a big bang. A founding blow in which the universe is embryonic, it precedes the expansion in the universal, space has already received this before receiving the things themselves, it has already formed the space where the things are going to be lodged. I am assuming that there was no big bang, that original cosmological preconcept; I am assuming that there was and still is an inaccessible number of different noises.

There is no silence in a strict sense. There are black boxes, but there is no *camera surda*. If old Cain had fled from God's speech, he would have stopped his wanderings at once; he would have immediately realized that there are no walls or bulkheads impervious to puffs of air or the voice.

Noise, you see, is also the trace of the observer. There is noise in the subject, there is noise in the object. Meddling in the phenomenon, the receiver introduces or produces a certain noise there, his own, for no one can live without noise. The condition of his being a receiver, a subject, an observer, is, precisely, that he make less noise than the noise transmitted by the object observed. If he gives off more noise, it obliterates the object, covers or hides it. An immense mouth, miniscule ears, how many are thus built, animals in their misrecognition! Cognition is subtraction of the noise received and of the noise made by the subject.

There is noise in the subject, there is noise in the object. There is noise in the observed, there is noise in the observer. In the transmitter and in the receiver, in the entire space of the channel. There is noise in being and in appearing. It crosses the most prominent divisions of philosophy and makes a mockery of its criteria. It is in being and in knowing. It is in the real, and in the sign, already.

Noise has no contradictory. The contradiction of a noise is a noise. The *noise* has no contrary. The space of a *noise* has no complementary, no outside. Logic is drowned in the *noise*. Of the prelogical or the antepredicative I know only the noise. And the fury.

~

A murmur is not primal, as I've just said, it is only repeated. The primal noise, consequently, is: *Murs* [the French for walls]. Thus the djinns begin to form their compleat whirlwind, a true cone with two nappes, and those mural murmurings, those wailing walls are there only to tell the noises just prior to the murmurs. *Murs*, the atoms of murmurs, walls, the atoms of wails, walls, the atoms of noise.

~

There is no wall impervious to noise. There are walls impervious to vision or light, there are boxes of shadow, no one has ever found silent places.

The wall is there, a *mur*, the faintest noise has already passed through it. Or has stopped. No one knows.

Demons

Noise, again. The background noise is permanent, it is the ground of the world, the backdrop of the universe, the background of being, maybe.

This ruckus never stops, the pandemonium of the gray sea, the fringed tumult of things themselves in the hollow of sleep, the imperceptible stirring of detail in the quiet. Every particle is aquiver while all is asleep. All is dormant, yet all is wakeful.

Noises loom up, figures, shapes against this background. They appear and withdraw, take form and dissolve, grow and disappear by melting into the background.

Background noise, I believe, is not dependent on me, not dependent on anyone, it is permanent, it is there for all, it is the ground of space and time, what things are based upon.

Noises that come and go are contingent on an observer, they

hinge on a listening post, on a channel, on an aperture, open or closed, door or window, through which they pass in part, and behind which the one who is the receiver of the flux, the wind, the manifestation, takes refuge and trembles.

The sea is gray. I had thought the great multiplicity was white, I thought it was clamorous and blank, I thought it was the aquarian chaos, a laminar falls, and at the same time the open and turbulent chaos. The sea is gray, the sea is the two chaos together. Manifold *noise* means the white is gray. But that is only an appearance. There is no gray, strictly speaking. There is white, the sum of colors, there is noisiness, the totality of number. Gray is not a totality, it is only a manifestation of *noise,* or a phenomenon of whiteness. Gray is not a medium, between black and white. White is gray in its totality, black is gray too in its number. There is no half-gray.

At the entrance to the hall, they heard a noise. There arose, coming from the sky, a noise like an impetuous wind. They've moved on, their band takes off and flies on, and their feet have ceased banging at my door with their redoubled attacks. The noise stops, they are going away.

It comes from a direction, the sky, the door, the plain. On the plain a noise arises. Over by the port and the gray deep, the fractal breeze is casting the crest of the surge in all directions, as in the customary eternity, the numberless smile of that gale, everlasting.

It is coming toward me, in one way. Background noise, stable and unstable, does without sense, it is the non-sense of sense or the absence of sense, because it is going, locally, every which way: everything flies. Everything is going from everywhere in every direction and refracting everywhere.

On the plain a noise arises. A door and a direction, a semiconduction and a way, a receiver, a Maxwell's demon. The wind does not perhaps quite come whencesoever it will. In the beginning, then, is the bifurcation. Henceforth we shall always say: the instauration. In the beginning is the cross.

Behind the valve, behind the duct, the demon seems to tremble. He bends under the flux. He warps under the pressure. If he takes off, if he runs away, he is following a direction, in the same direction as direction, and, from now on, he is motionless, in the flux of the sense of direction, he is in the wind, he sees, hears no more. To be blind and deaf one need only follow the wind. The weathervane, unstable in point and direction, fluctuates in the background noise. But that isn't true, the weathervane resists the gale, it shows the point of the wind and its angle, it is a rudder, it steers. Being blank, it tells all directions, but at any given moment it has a single direction.

In making the wind manifest and taking the point, the blade of the rudder trembles and vibrates. It trembles all over, it is afraid, with good reason; it is afraid, because it is trembling, and it is trembling because it points the way, that toward which the flux is hurrying. What the flux is hurrying toward is the receiver, which is not yet certain to let it pass through.

Immersed in background noise with its fractal agitation, the observer attracts the directional flux. It comes toward him, it is bound to. Should there be some wind, it will blow in his direction, any other point, for him, will be in the background. Immersed in disorder, all order is directed toward him. Toward him, at him, and against him.

Knowledge is, first of all, terrifying. It is rushing at us.

It rushes around. In disorder where, necessarily, the observer loses his senses and his bearings, he wakes up, if he wakes up, in a bed, a channel, a flux, a flow. Everything was running away, everything is running away, in the background noise, and, now, everything is flowing.

It comes from upstream in relation to me, it comes windward to me. But I am not sure, before the actual meeting, that it will flow downstream, leeward to me. I become the observer only if the course passes under my window, from upstream to downstream, and from windward to leeward, only if the noise passes in front of my door.

Should it stop, I am the victim. I am dead. Impaled by the flux, blown through by the wind, nailed by the arrow. The wall buckles.

The point, which I point to, arrowed in my direction, frightens me.

If there is no observer, or if the observer dies, the vortex is a demi-cone, as with calumny, Beaumarchais. If there is an observer and if he is safe, the vortex is complete, cones inverted at their base, as with the djinns, Hugo. The case of death and the case of survival.

~

Background noise has no shore, is it infinite, I don't know, in any case, it is not finite. The sharp, piercing signal of the bell, the jingle bell or the cry, is a unitary and solitary sound. It pierces time in an instant. Its arrow flieth by day. The noise that makes itself felt from afar and rises toward me like a surging swell before it is lost is pure multiplicity. It is rumor. A rumor is not pandemonium, it is not an uproar. The background noise is always there, the signal claps like a flash of lightning, *rumor* rushes forth. The signal is a unit, pandemonium is undefined, rumor is a plurality. The ruckus fluctuates, like choppy waters lapping, the signal is a fluctuation, the rumor's noise is the flux, or the totality of fluxions. It increases, decreases, globally, locally it is multiple, various, variegated. Voices, cries, tears, thunderings, rumblings, whistles and crashes, breaths, blasts, grindings, blows, chains and beats, cracklings and sounds, growling and waves, moans that die away . . . the river of noise carries along a thousand tonalities.

The differential of the flux is fluxion. So the flux is a sum, and classical rationality is safe, I am going from the local, fluxion, to the global, flux, and conversely. Be advised: flux is a multiplicity of fluctuations. So flux is unintegrable, it is not a sum, the path from the global to the local and back can be cut. I am praying for a completely new calculus for fluctuations, a different rationality remains to be conceived.

~

Rumor rushes forth, it is a crowd.

This noise against me hurls headlong, a crowd is rushing at me.

I am not Maxwell's demon, yet; them, those in the crowd, they alone are the demons. The demons from a strange ritual, oriental, so they say. Imaginary, to be sure, gruesome vampires, a hideous army of dwarfs and dragons, a hell of foul demons with clawed wings.

A crowd, *turba*, whirls around me, *turbo*, and disturbs me.

~

A crowd, a swarm, an army, a herd, a battalion, the pitched multiplicity, howling and motley with shouts, rushes toward us, rushes toward me, toward me alone, me the victim, bowed down, safe, tomorrow, before the altars.

The noises of space, the colors of the world are coming toward me. I am plunged here and now in colors and noises to the point of dizziness. Here and now means that a flux of noises and colors is coming at me. I am a semiconductor, I admit it, I am the demon, I pull among the multiplicity of directions the direction that, from some upstream, comes at me.

This crowd comes at me, it threatens to knock me down, to trample me, to throw me under it. Then and only then am I a subject. I am thrown under the multiple. Prostrate beneath the waves of noise, I am a castaway of perception. I am swallowed up in space, drowned in its murmuring, the multiple always overflows me. I am a subject only when I am on the verge of fainting, dying.

In other words: the crowd comes at me, the mob knocks me down, dismembers me, cuts me up, I am going to see the open heavens.

Knowledge is born of this danger of death.

~

Just now calumny was covering space with a growing torment. Through multiplied bifurcations, the vortex was being born, was being amplified to its totality. Turbulence was described to some extent from the point of view of God, I mean of the sociologist. The dark or gray tide of dwarfs coming from the seaside to drown my house, the tsunami, the whirlwind are described under the dictation of the subject himself, from the point of view of the dead man, the subject who risks death in the face of the flux. Fear, hideousness, vampires, dragons, the multiple, at first, inspire fear. It comes from the calumny or the foul demons of the night. What terrifies is not the meaning of the noise—the thing spoken, forspoken—but the increasing multiplicity that says it. Fear comes from the swarming, the tide, the dread multiplies like flies, knowledge through concepts regiments this nauseous herd under the pure generality of the one. The concept is reassuring at first, it represses the press of the crowd. Rationality was born of this terror.

Rationality buries empiricism alive. It dispatches Protagoras to Hades. But these demons are nothing but the calls of the world, or the moans of the others who are crying for help. Would you be frightened by this wailing?

Vortex

The mur-mur has passed through the wall.

All is nought: death, sleep, and the night. The plain.

Background noise is settled in this blank nullity: the breeze breathes.

Listen: what is born amidst the noises of breath, in the midst of the breath settled in the blank whiteness of the plain, what is born ought to be a signal. Like a signal high upon the barbed noise, indistinct, as little differentiated as the plain itself. Yet no, it is not a signal, it is a noise still. The repetitive background noise is the gray deep and the breathing breeze. What is born, soul, flame, jingle bell, what is born from the blank is a dance, and the dance of a dwarf, as tiny as the lapping in the breeze's smile. The signal would be high upon the waves, the dwarf is low like the other waves, not distinguishable from them. The dwarf is dancing at the tip of a surge, see his foot upon the noisy sea.

The dwarf's foot leaping, dashing, the dwarf's foot littler than the little dwarf, is a fraction of the dancing wave, the foot at the tip of the surge, the tip of the crest of the swell, now *that* is what a fluctuation is.

The noise, gray deep and breeze that breathes, the noise, the surge, is a multiplicity of which we do not know the sum. We do not know how to integrate it in a sound, a sense, a harmony, we do not have a concept for it. The second noise, the noise that is born, as a noise lodged in the noise, a noise in its turn settled in the blankness of space, that second noise is not a fluxion, a tiny little meaning, a local concept, a tiny little god in his little department, a miniature, a scaled-down model. No, it is not a fluxion, it is a fluctuation. The dwarf, the djinn, is neither man nor petty god, it is a misshapen being, a shadow, a vampire, a crane, a dragon, claws in its wings, a locust. You never see it full-size, a dwarf will not get bigger. Natural language has long been admirably expressing these inchoative, frequentative forms, with which scholarly rationality, a bit pedestrian, has difficulty catching up. Our language leaps and dances, rationality walks in step. Every step is alike, a fluxion, every leap, every fluctuation maintains its singularity.

The fluctuation passes through the mesh of bifurcations. Hopping on one leg. Even the *belle noiseuse* lets only one foot be seen, the other one is in the air, absent. Hopping on one leg: like the sound of a crowd thundering and rolling, now collapsing, now getting bigger. Our dovetail is back again, our instauration, and the old poisonous stroke. Everything starts all over again, at every step the fluctuation makes a choice, here at every strophe, catastrophe, either to die or to get bigger.

~

The djinns are familiar with the physics of Lucretius, they are particles of noise, jolts, tips of flames, jingle bells. Ill individuated, dragons or locusts? Badly congregated, a herd, a swarm, a cloud, barely aggregated. Undefined locally, globally they go further than Lucretian physics. But their cloud, flying in the empty space, the noise of scattershot in the blank silence, carries a lightning flash at its flank.

The flash of lightning steers the universe. The blade of rudder bifurcates to the left, to the right with its dovetail. There is inclination. The lightning forks, it inclines, a zigzag.

The roofbeam is bent, the wall bows and the house is tottering. The roofbeam is slanting, the house is slanting. The *mur*, the wall, the first noise repeated by the echo, the *mur*, the wall, the first obstacle, the fragile auricle, the wall assumes the warp and bends.

See inclination everywhere.

~

The expansive fizzle of sea noise is broken up into fluctuations. A given one of them, dwarfish, singular begins gathering followers. Why? We do not know. A thousand, a hundred thousand, unique, have started out, no doubt, and then collapsed into the stillness of the noise, washed out by the *noise*. A thousand, a hundred thousand, others having made two or three dovetails, returned to the gray deep and the breeze. So many little flashes fading rapidly away, so many whisperings rising, I thought I heard a call in the uproar, a signal amid the pandemonium, the wave, heaving up a moment, falls again. Why is that one, that unique one, not lost? Answer: why were the others, those unique ones, lost?

A head emerges from the crowd, eyes, mouth, neck, perhaps even from time to time the shoulders. A few heads, here and there, emerge and, with their barely open eyes, seem to look at that mouth, be amazed, and let their own gape wide in their turn, is this a phenomenon on its way, like a chorus heralding itself, no, everything has gone back to the choppy brief swell, and this happens a hundred times a day. Is background noise a welter of aborted beginnings? Is it messages only half spoken? The clinking cacophonic collision of unaddressed bottles in the sea? Hear multiply how the immense things that our pretension calls history commence. Conceive conceptionless how time can begin.

～

The wall assumes the warp and bends, it inclines.

The echo repeats the voice, the noise rolls like a wave. The inclination was the onset of the turning motion, the spiral of the vortex is its upshot. Let us flee beneath the spiral of the deep winding stair.

We do not really know how this turning motion takes place. Repetitiveness is necessary for it. A fluctuation is repeated, or it encounters, by chance, the same. An echo is necessary for it, in things, and imitation, among men. Redundancy is necessary for it. It enters noise. These are the first of the forms of order: redundancy, repetition, echo, imitation. An echo in the case of rumor, a mimetic act in the case of fury. No circle without a return of the same.

Our languages have always heard, have always expressed well the wheeling force and its return upon itself. Rhythm is a fluctuation of the rhesis, the surge. The dwarf called a djinn is falsely Arabian, I hear him whisper in Greek. The Greek language recognizes that a fragment of the outflow may flow, circulate. But French also knows as much. Rhythm is no more mysterious than our cadence. A cadence, a fragment of a fall, a fluctuation of decadence, cadence turns back what seems irreversible. The flowing flux turns through rhythm, and what falls comes back on itself in cadence. Our natural languages have paid attention to an order formed through a fall or a flowing out, among the noises of the waters, and in unexpected, chaotic conditions.

These languages dance, in cadence, at the edge of the noise, they come from it, and they return to it, they turn back on themselves. To arise from the primal noise, they need repetitiveness, an echo, a rhythm, redundancy. In the beginning is the echo: murmur.

~

When languages talk about themselves, they begin the circle again. They come from rumor in a whirlwind. First through echo, repetition. Then through redundancy. Then through rhythm and cadence. These circles follow one another every which way. The unexpected feeds the circle that maintains the unexpected and acclimates it to the predictable, thus does the turbulence get bigger. When languages know how to talk about themselves, they only create a further circle. Any metalanguage closes the loop of another course, slightly shifted, to be sure, but of the same form as those first little rhythmic poems. Metaphysics comes from the same whirlwind as music. Reflection, at whatever level, is a loop, sameness and different, in the whirling whole of the organization of languages by themselves. The more one knows how to talk about languages, the better languages know how to talk. As long, of course, as they continue to hear the noise.

~

The swarm wheels, hissing, the multiple rolls, whirling. The poem in the form of a double cone has the shape of the vortex. The nascent form of language, the nascent form of Aphrodite, the form of any nascent phenomenon, bodies, things, signs.

The Chain

Here then is the chain: white sea or white plain, background noise, surge, fluctuation of the surge, bifurcation, repetition, rhythm or cadence, vortex. The great turbulence is constituted, it fades away, it breaks. And disappears as it came.

This chain is breaking, it is breaking at every point, it may always break, its characteristic is to snap. It is fragile, unstable.

This chain is not the chain of reasons, simple and easy. Easy: in other words, reliable. The chain of reasons is reliable because it is reduced to the law of the weakest link, and thus in any other linkage there is always more than enough strength. It is reliable through the law of the slowest actuating force, and because there is consequently more than enough speed in any other linkage. On the global chain of circulation, everybody understands that the fastest speed is that of the slowest party. The weakest and slowest are the general law here. Everywhere else, consequently, there are residues, surplus stocks. The chain is solid because it has surplus stocks all over, except at one point, where it can break. These reserves everywhere ensure linkage and stability.

The chain conceived here has the essential attribute of being able to break at all points and at all times. In actuality, it almost always fades away, almost everywhere, in actuality it dies right in the vicinity of being born. It begins and it has an almost infinitesimally brief life. Calls, little signals, lights, and then fading in the mist. A long form that seems lively until adolescence and vanishes almost at the same time as its counterparts. The links of the chain of reasons are strongly joined in proportion as the surplus, the difference between the strongest and the weakest, is great. The links of the weakest do not connect, do not catch, they touch. They touch, they are tangential. This is the chain of contingency. *No, the contingent chain does not break, its links slide over one another, as though viscous. They touch because they are adjacent, they touch like sailors' hitches or the loops of motorway cloverleaves are stacked upon one another. It is not a linkage, but a local pull, by way of little frictions. The local pull induces a global movement very seldom, although it can happen. This is not a solid chain, it is simply a liquid movement, a viscosity, a propagation that wagers its age in each locality. Here we are in liquid history and the ages of waters.*

It is the chain of genesis. *It is not solid. It is never a chain of necessity. Suddenly, it will bifurcate. It goes off on a tangent. It surrenders to the passing signals, the fluctuations of the sea, or some sowing of sameness. This chain is not a chain of chance either, it would remain meticulously broken. It is a chain of contingency, the recruiting takes place through tangency, by local pulls and by degrees, by word of mouth, from one mouth to another. It emerges from the sea noise, the nautical noise, the prebiotic soup.*

A fragile and soft chain, easily cut, fragments easily replaced, a chain almost always broken, almost everywhere and always decreasing, here and there increasing slightly, increasing here suddenly crazily, it invades space, it occupies, it covers the place, but only temporarily. It is the chain of life.

It must be an element of the drives and pulls of nature, it is a bit of life's secret, a series of sudden and risky leaps of thought that can invent, throw itself into the noise, support itself in redundancy, a long piece of melody, sometimes rhythmic, in tempo as it were, sometimes letting go, as by a free end, some proposition that is aperiodical but right.

It is a little bit of the secret thrust of our awakenings, and the timid and green advance of the new. Look at it: it is the dance of time, which is dormant in our habitual behavior.

~

This discourse, I am not afraid of the fact, is original, it is even the origin of language in noise. This discourse is weak and fragile, neighboring on silence. Most often it collapses back into the background noise. Robust in rebirth, almost everywhere stillborn. This chain is naturing, it is almost never natured. Always blinking and never steady. Just as attracted by death as by birth. An original discourse, perhaps, but its beginnings are only attempts.

The stable chain of the rationalists only expresses, I think, their desire of domination. The empire is never more than some inflated local, a part that took the place of the whole. The local, by its inflation, fills space with its redundancy. The law of the serial is repeated in every link, the place grows step by step. Soon order rules without exception. There is reason there, there is violence there. There is order and growth there. To be sure there is a great deal of intelligence there, no one could measure it, yet there is invasion there as well. Immeasurable. The little pyramid grows, the medium one is still growing, the large one shows that a larger one can be built, and soon the world's space will be in the tomb of an immense transparent and burning pyramid. This chain is a chain of reason, this chain is a chain of death. The union of measure and growth, similitude and invasion, conservation and redundancy, is the union of reason and death itself.

My predecessors were fascinated by dominating reason, the clerical alliance of empire and ideas, of which the chain of reasons was the emblem and the tool. The growth of the pyramids crystallizes the space of the world, it vitrifies it. Nothing new under the fire of these tombs. They loved only ideas occupying the universal. That isn't intelligence. They loved only the order fit to invade the world. That isn't invention or science. They never loved anything but repetition. The dream of a predatory bird whose cries would not be answered by the cries of any other bird, the nightmare of a single niche.

I have understood at last why the endeavor that was no doubt born in the classical era had to end in the Los Alamos desert, at the place where all the grains of sand look alike, where the work of men still vitrifies them. Rationalism is a vehicle of death. Science must dissociate itself from it.

The soft quasi-chain conjured up here, glimpsed, sketched, faintly, its local, tangential, contingent, aquatic drives and pulls, its open, free and unstable links, this badly woven fabric, or these proximities almost always abandoned as trials, attempts, essays, hold true, I believe, on occasion, for the inert, more often for the living, little for the pathological and sometimes for the cultural, they hold true, I believe, for history. These small propagations, which are endlessly zebra-streaking the background noise drift into, do not drift into, can sometimes drift into the universal.

~

The one who used to receive the army of shouts head-on has retreated. We shall not be seeing his body dead in the center of the largest circle. He was with Beaumarchais, under the chorus of hatred and proscription. The subject is not dead. The noise is on its way, at the edge of the horizon, it will seek its fortune elsewhere, in the world.

Noise, through bifurcations and metamorphoses, occupied space. It finds a bifurcation. It hesitates. It comes back to its dark side, to the night. Bifurcation: space effaces the noise. One invariant covers over the other.

~

Life has disappeared as it came, like a world, like a signal or a thought. The pure multiple caused turbulence, it returns to multiplied ashes. Everything dies.

Aphrodite turbulent, immense in space, has vanished like a vapor. The fluid vortex has evaporated.

Exodus

To take a place or to give up a place, that is the whole question. There are those who take places, there are those who give them up. Those who take places take places always and everywhere, and those who give up places always do so. There are places taken, there are no unoccupied places. Space consists of, and is saturated with places taken, and in them swarm restless, almost motionless, the takers. The restlessness comes from the struggle for place. All space is noisy, clamorous, it is a cloud, a chaos, under the martial and stable law of noise and combat. It may at a moment be order under the law of the strongest. But one must make more noise than the others in order for one's shout of *no more noise* to be heard and for the others to obey. One must demonstrate more fury to strike fear into fury. Neither noise nor fury ever ceases, even under the dominion of those who claim to eliminate them. The latter have simply monopolized the *noise.* The whole of space, breach by breach, has been parasitized. The painting of *La Belle Noiseuse,* where the girl is blent under fury and noise, is the space of parasites, interferences. The path that would lead us to see her is saturated with obstacles. When space is parasitized, there are only two solutions. One can seize the place shouting *death to the parasite.* And this is the solution of the parasite, for a parasite is put to death only by a stronger parasite. And the place has not changed in nature. Or one can give the place up and flee. To take a place or to give up a place, that is the whole question.

Those who are taking the places are in a stable position, for they lean on those who hold them. Places are attacked tooth and nail by the takers, defended tooth and nail by the holders. The perfect symmetry of the struggle, the gemination of the controversy, the unstable and stable equilibrium of the strong weighing down on the stronghold, the force fighting against the counterforce and leaning on it, define place. They struggle to hold the place that is defined by their struggle. Everybody says of them that they are the movers of history, because they appear to expend a lot of energy, because they make a lot of noise. Let's look at where the energy goes. It may be consumed in producing. I speak of its surplus, what is not set aside for survival. Energy is not always expended for the sake of production. Often it is diverted. It is drained into combat, into shouts and fury. I think that struggle is to production, in terms of hardware or high energies, what a cry is to language, in terms of software or low energies. Noise on the one hand, wrangling on the other, *noise* in a nutshell, are parasitic. They are parasites, they are produced by the parasites, they attract parasites in droves. The diversion in question diverts things' attention onto the spectacle and representation. The parasites swoop down in droves on the product and the producer, until they are concealed. It is not the beauty, *la belle,* perhaps, that makes the *noise:* the great recumbent body of this beauty is lost like a carcass under millions of helminths. It looks like the belly of sleeping Gulliver moving under the feverish activity of thousands of Lilliputians. The beautiful woman is devoured by these little creatures. And it is not the naked beauty that attracts attention, everyone forgets Gillette, it is the bitter struggle of the beasts.

Fighting and making noise are all it takes to attract the attention of a third party, and to make up a spectacle and spectators, thus goes history. It draws the observer into this representation. Soon, he will be on fire to get his share, he will want to participate, he will want to take a place. No, it is not Gillette alive, naked and real, loving, that attracts attention, it is the *noise* and the diverted energy, the parasitic interference, the representation. The naked woman or desire is less attractive than the brawl. The *noise* is so enthralling that Poussin and Porbus, a thousand others and us too, we scrutinize its smallest peculiarities. Although the rule is dopey and dull: whoever is on a place is hated by another place-taker and instead of making room, producing a place, they fight and then a third party intrigued by the spectacle comes forward, and he wants the place and instead of producing a place, he fights to take it, and the combat underway attracts a fourth who ... The passion for history is thus a part of history, it does not even allow the dead to bury the dead, thus does Gillette weep to see her lover melt away, through attention and staring, in the *noise* of noise, color, representation, and hatred. And representation is hatred, someone takes the place of someone else. And I hate you already, she says, already starting to enter into it a bit, setting her naked foot into the corner of the painting. The old madman's painting is a formidable well of attraction, the *noise* is a vertigo of seduction, it has the form of a vortex, who can say he is exempt from it, the painting is the place of those who take places, it is the place of all those who, through their struggles and their noise, define place, it is thus the place of all places, and I know now what the real title of this painting is: the human comedy. Or, if you wish, the drama of history. For the law of history is *noise*. An unknown masterpiece in the series of known masterpieces, a subset well defined in the noisy ocean of Balzac's pages, where we can read, without having dominion over it, the law of the aggregate.

Those who take the places are unstable and stable. They create motion and rest. They appear to be in motion and they are at rest. Their movements define places, and are resolved into rest. They appear to be fighting, they are leaning on one another. They appear to be agitating, they are agitated. The whole of the swarming is equal to nullity. No, they do not do nothing, but they fake doing. Faking, appearance, representation are not nothing. They are not slacking, they are faking. Representation, faking, no, they aren't nothing. They cover the body of the beauty, cover the referent, cover the process of production, all this swarming parasitical interference covers the real body. The history of *noise* covers, with its *noise*, history. In a nutshell, it takes its place. It is easy to sum up the little functions and the little local pseudo-labors of all those who struggle to take and to define the little local places. The totality is to take a place, and that is all. They are the substitutes. They are the *lieu-tenants*, the place-holders. Literally, they are the representatives. For every representation presupposes that someone is placed in the place of someone else. The struggle for place is therefore purely and simply a representational struggle. The struggle and the fight, all of polemics, all of dialectics, all relation between forces have as their initial presupposition, as their result, this change, this trading of place. They are thus all plunged in the phenomenon, in phenomenology—in appearance. In the appearance and illusion of movement, action, history. The illusion of a mover of the illusion of history. The painting is the royal place of a comic illusion, the illusion of the human comedy.

~

The more they hate, the more they fight, the more they kill one other, the more they sink, immobilized, in illusion, the more they thicken the great wall of appearance.

History, immobile, is buried beneath the noisy turbulence.

Those who are taking the places remain stable through exchange and substitution, by changing-of-the-guard and lieutenancy. Dialectics comes down to a combinatory apparatus. The one doesn't get any further than the other. And through substitution, there is only murder and appearance.

Those who give up their places, move and flow. Their blankness is pure processuality. To yield means to take a step. To step aside, we say. Those who step aside, those who cede their place, begin, by their cession, a process. Those who take the places stabilize them and drown them in *noise.* Those who give up their place have already taken a step. On the chaotic and noisy painting, then, can be seen the trace of a step and the print of the foot, alive, of the one who just gave up the place. Each billow of the Albula makes way for each billow from upstream, and each billow downstream in turn makes way for it. The smooth billowing Albula is not turbulent.

Those of the blank place are advancing. They have just stepped aside. The only steps are steps aside. There is no step that is not a cession. Those who give up their place yield it up to all those who take places, they yield it to everyone, they always yield it. They never have a place to put their foot down, they never have a place to rest their head, they have no rest. They are always moving. There is no movement except by stepping aside, giving up one's place. Thus, the series of cessions makes process. As soon as they find, discover, invent a blank place, the clamorous noisemakers who take the places race in, invade it, pin it down with noise, fury, hatred and illusion, they bury it beneath their tumult, and the original ones give up the place. The blank place is the place of the continuous cession. There is no blank white place, there are only the blank white ones who step aside. There is no blank place, there is only a blank step, the step of giving up a place, there is only a trace of a step, that white foot, exquisite, alive, in the midst of the *noise*.

Do not say: no man is a prophet in his own country, that's just a banality. Say rather, such a one was obliged to become a prophet, as soon as he gave up his place in his native land.

There are no invaders, there are only people who have given up their place. There are no conquerors, there are excluded ones, banished ones, in search of a place. Those who are moving forward have just given up a place and they come upon a place held by place-holders. Pay attention to those who give way, for they are the ones who are on the move. Any displacement is their deed. They are the very displacement themselves. Driven out, expelled from the first place, remember our first parents. The thesis is on the spot, and the antithesis backs it up: rest and thesis anew through a little shift of readjustment in the balance. Thesis and antithesis, through *noise*, provide synthesis at rest, in equilibrium. But this work of the negative drives out, banishes, excludes the middle, the third position. The third position that is not attracted by the *noise*, the third gives up the place, becomes dis-placed. There has only ever been any true displacement outside of the relationship of the thesis and antithesis: like the angel with a flaming sword and the seductive spirit of evil, they hold the first place, will not leave it, are there in a stable equilibrium. History began with a similar expulsion. We are the children of those who gave up the place. We are the children in history of those who stepped aside. We are all children of exiles. The whole of culture is this excluded third.

The *belle noiseuse* is now beautiful Helen herself. Troy is a first place, the beautiful capital. Set ablaze and a-bleeding in fury, murder and noise. Aeneas, vanquished, steps aside. Ulysses, triumphant, also steps aside. There they both are fleeing over the noisy sea. Blank Ulysses, lissome Ulysses, Nobody Ulysses subject of thought, travels. Never is he the daring seaman who explores places and regions, never is he the conqueror, the invader, the courageous navigator who discovers regions and invents places, he is always chased out of the region, and he gives up the place.

He leaves. He parts from islands and shores, he flees before time. He escapes from the pen of the den under the fleecy abdomen of the buck. His journey is not foreseen, not deliberate, not as they say, programmed, his journey is undergone. Ulysses escapes from women. His route is not methodical, his path is always exodical. Outside of the place and off the route. He again passes by known lands, he marvels at the unknown places because he is pushed out of bounds, off the beaten track, subjected to meteors. He didn't want it. He stepped aside. His vessel yields to the pressures of turbulence. Blank Ulysses is himself alone the whole of the Hebrew people. It has just been driven out of Egypt. It wanted to leave Egypt. The Hebrew people steps aside. It becomes blank like the white desert. Blank like a blank page. The Hebrew people endure their exodus and the traces of their steps mark the white desert. Moses left the places, Moses will not rest in his place. Moses is blank, he is the tabula rasa of the law on which Jehovah writes. God writes history on the Hebrew people who step aside, as a choreographer writes the ballet on the transparent body of the dancer, who steps aside. The dancer who dances so as to step aside. Who leaves a place. Dance is a step that leaves a place. Aeneas, beaten, steps aside and leaves a place. He roams the Mediterranean, exodus. He wanders like Gilgamesh, like Ulysses, like the Hebrew people. An exodus at sea, on land, or in the desert. He is a little bit Greek, a little Semitic after his visit to Dido in Carthage, he is going to be Roman. We are, through history, sons of those who made history or invented history in giving up their place. We are the children of the exodus, the Hebrew exodus, the Odyssean exodus, the Aeneid exodus, exoduses landing on the banks of the Albula. We are all children of exiles, children of meanderings. The exodus gives up its place, steps aside, and goes off course, it becomes a meandering. The meander leaves the *noise*. Meandering always gets out of *noise*. *Noise* is the sign of places. The more places there are, the more *noise* there is; the more *noise* there is, the more places there are. There is no space without noise nor any noise without space. Battle is the sign of the space to be taken, noise is its call. Sound and fury are the masters of places, consequently, they are the bleak iteration of the same thesis, its equilibrium returning, conserved. The excluded third leaves the *noise*, is always trying to. The third seeks a completely blank space, finds it on rare occasions. The miracle of flat projection space doesn't happen every morning. The miracle of a space without *noise* is rare. The exile gives up his place, he throws himself into the exodus, knowing only his cession. He cedes at every step. His unpredictable course is a meandering. His quantum of information is tremendous. Those of the *noise*, of noise and polemics, appear to manipulate rich stores of information, when in fact they are immersed in redundancy. The form of the squabble is stable and perennial. There is nothing in all that noise. The unpredictable meandering unlocks knowledge for Ulysses, history for the Hebrew people, opens Rome for Aeneas. Polemic is always predictable. One always hears the same uproar in it. We are the children of those meanderings, sons of the wandering Jews, sons of the wandering Greeks, sons of the wandering Trojans. The founding of Rome concludes these exoduses in a blank page, the city of Alba and its white river.

~

Aeneas, son of Venus, hail.

Aphrodite belongs to love, for having lēft the *noise*.

4

The Birth of Time

HEROIC FURIES
   CLASSES
      QUASI-OBJECTS

     PROCESS

      CHAOS, JOLTS, MOB
       THE WORK OF THE MULTIPLE
        INTERMITTENCES
         SOLIDS, FLUIDS
          MIX
           TIME

In the matter of the history of religions, in the matter of sociology, perhaps in the matter of anthropology, we have just now passed the point where Linnaeus, the classifier, can be reconsidered in the manner of Darwin, the evolutionist. I am speaking through images. The age of invariance is replaced by the age of variation. The structural system and Georges Dumézil's comparative method lead to classification. They help identify among Indo-Europeans of every branch the invariability of three classes or social functions: sovereignty, struggle, and production. Jupiter, Mars, and Quirinus, under different names, in diverse places, remain the gods of these peoples, in their religion, their philosophy, their history, and their assembly. We do not contest these findings, by which we have been instructed and gratified, I would to God that our youth encountered only these kinds of masters.

Nevertheless, and now, I think that the invariance of these three classes is not of the essence, and I will attempt to demonstrate as much.

Heroic Furies

Let us consider one of these classes, the one whose effigy is Mars, the military. Dumézil's book on Horace and the Curiatii has, as of 1942, brought it to light and put it in place. We are still mulling this book over, though we are taking it for granted all the same. Right from the beginning, it is about fury. Strictly faithful to the things themselves, fury is the best way into the problem. Yes, fury is a state often described in narratives of reference; yes, fury is a principle that cuts across the three functions, it presides over mystical ecstasies, sovereign magicks, over the unleashed savagery of the mercenaries, over the orgies of drinking and sex in festivals of productivity. In this, then, fury is not classed, in this fury is anterior to the tripartition. The author even terms it—a principle of human action. I shall thus assume that, unclassed itself, fury is classing, I shall assume that it is an energy which, in its course, becomes frozen, rises in tiers and is structured in classes and functions. I take this book seriously, I take seriously the origin it sets up and displays, that terrifying origin.

Classes are a result of fury, provided that the word and the thing be reconsidered. Fury is not only the state of a warrior heating up for battle, it is also a magical and orgiastic state. It does not belong to Mars. Listen, this is new. The military man is not, within the group, the lone specialist marked by violence. The *noise* is not the soldier's business alone, he is not the only one affected by it. The priest is just as much involved, and so is the politician, be he king or tribune, the manufacturer shoulders it, too. Fury is distributed among the three classes: it is not individual, but collective. It does not belong to the hero alone, but to his group, it does not belong to the group alone, but to the whole of society. Classes were invariants of Indo-European space and time, they remain so, fury, in its turn, is the invariant of these classes. It is inevitable that these classes become its result. Fury is a classifier.

Fury is not only a matter of Mars, it is a matter of Jupiter, and of Quirinus as well. It is not the state of one man, solely, it is a recognized state of the group, the crowd, the collective. The population, let loose, ravages everything in its path, and that is the Latin meaning of the word *population*, the ravaging masses. The *noise* is only rarely a duel, *noise* is the multiple's. We have experienced the restless agitation of the multitude, unconstrained, on rare occasions, most often in a ritualized state. For a long time I believed that history was producing it before thinking that it was producing history. It has been acknowledged by some authors, rather well described by Lucretius or Zola, enlisted by Canetti, admirably limned by Homer, Livy, Shakespeare, the Greek and French writers of tragedies. *Noise* and fury are the tragic driving force. In this noisy state, free energy is diffused, it increases crazily, it suddenly abates and stabilizes. It is frozen in institutions, organizations, functions.

Hobbes's term for the original social state is: the war of all against all. It seems to me that the word *war* is not right. War is decided, it is declared, ordered, prepared, institutionalized, made sacred, it is won, lost, concluded by treaty. War is a state of order, a classic state of lines and columns, maps and strategies, leaders and spectacle, it knows friends, enemies, neutrals, allies, it defines belligerence. Sadly, I now believe that war is a cure for violence, I think that a duel, a pitched battle, confrontation, dialectic are all veils over violence. They are encounters, matches, representations, they are not brawls. Sadly. The primal state, the primitive state, before any contract, is a pre-ordered state, undecided, undeclared, unprepared for, not stabilized in institutions. No, it is not war, it is *noise;* no, it is not war, it is the multitude in a fury. The multiple, in each point not defined, each having lost any principle of individuation, as in drunkenness or unanimous communion, the multiple undefined globally, a group, a crowd, a population, an underworld, in short, everything that the Suburra or the Ergastulum spew up, each time listen to the scornful words used by the one who does not understand or is loath to understand, the multiple gives itself as such: either it has lost the one or it has won for losing it. This war, misnamed by Hobbes, here called the *noise,* does not follow the classifications, this war, here called fury, precedes them. It is not classed, it classes. A society makes war to avoid at all costs the return to that state. The advantage of having at one's borders an hereditary enemy is immense. So is that of having a dialectic in one's logic. It allows one to remain comfortably within the concept, never to contemplate multiplicity. A contract, a covenant, holds fast the free energy of fury, perhaps, but would there be a contract, a covenant, any agreement without the energy of that *noise,* would there be a code without coding fury?

I take seriously the lesson of Girard, after that of Georges Dumézil. The Latin *furor,* I note, is related to the Greek θυω. Fury, I believe, is in precession over sacrifice. The multiple hurls itself headlong upon the one and surrounds it, this is the birth of the concept. The population swoops down upon the individual, fury moves onto the hero: it is the birth of tragedy, of collective culture, of logic, indeed, of the concept in general.

Classes

Let us go beyond antiquity, anthropology is as good as its word. According to theories, classical ever since the nineteenth century, social violence is to be had through class struggle. Fury here is the product of classes. Violence is secondary, classes are primary. They are also a matter of invariance. Well, in sociology, as in biology, in biology as in any classification, of sciences, beings, stones or numbers, classes are not essences. Whether they're present in nature or just through our knowledge, they remain products. In other words, the class has itself a history and a makeup, the classing has itself a history. To believe that class struggle is the driving force of history is to believe that class is outside of history, it is to say that classing remains eternitary. This cannot be the case. Class is in history and so is struggle, the driving force is elsewhere. To believe that class struggle is the driving force of history is, with exemplary rigor, to remain an Aristotelian.

We can imagine the reason for this division. When a system expands, in dimension, number, and complexity, it always has a tendency to form into subsets, having all the more distinction the larger the expansion, all the more specialized thereby, all the more separate the more the system tends to maintain its cohesion. This theorem is the general rule, all that remains is to look for exceptions or singularities. Therefore a class is constituted at a given moment in order to avoid the global unity being undone.

It is not originary, it must be a threshold effect. This description, although a function of time, remains static. It is difficult to see why this is so. I wish to show, once more in this, that the driving force is fury. A class is a threshold effect in the global expansion of the system, a class is also and above all, in its constitution, a strategic formation in relation to violence. Division into subsets minimizes fury. Division into subsets protects, preserves the unity of the body as a whole, because it tempers this free energy and channels it. Contrary to what the classical theory leads one to believe, class struggle does not produce energy, nor is it for that very reason a step forward, it minimizes and stabilizes them. If it were as classical theory has it, that theory would have discovered perpetual motion: products of history producing in turn, the history that produced them. Class in fact constitutes itself in relation to violence. It constitutes itself, within the group, as the group constituted itself, in its beginnings, within its own environment.

Let us recapitulate: Mars is not the sole trace of fury, in the social body as a whole. Jupiter is one as well, and so too is Quirinus. The three classes are traces of fury. I shall show it to you elsewhere. The paradox seems heavy-handed, but it makes sense: the military is a solution to the problem of violence, just as the priests and the economists are. Each shows its rationality in the face of an outbreak. Hence a fine appearance of the concrete: economy passes for reality, but it is no more real than theological discourse or patriotic eloquence. It is a parallel solution. Even more: any division into subsets is a solution of the same kind. Not because it heralds God or the King, the Motherland in danger, inflation or economic crisis, but because it is, simply, purely, a division. The division into classes is carried out under the pressure of a great danger, this danger's name is fury. I shall thus no longer say class struggle, but classes born of struggle. Try to put yourself outside of class and you will very soon see for yourself that the wind is much more violent on that plain than when sheltered by the group. I know very few exceptions to this martial law: everyone, with a shiver, snuggles back up with a pressure group, a class. And if a class were to speed up the struggle and the violence, it would very shortly be an empty class.

Thus, each class enjoys the privileges of all classes. All are sovereign and all are sacred, all profess themselves productive. They are protected by an aura of magic, religion, strength, and effects of concreteness. They produce unities, through them unity appears in the place and stead of multiplicities, they code. Coding is nothing more than showing unities in the stead of multiplicitary *noise*. Thus are concepts born.

~

We read, in Livy, the outbreak of the multitude, the clamors of the populace. We hear the naked collective fury, surrounded by the collective fury of enemies. The plebes are classed through exploitation, through debts, and if they liberate themselves from their bonds, they are in danger of going beyond their class. Soon this multitude becomes multitude once again, straggling, inflamed, blurred, unclassable. The whole task of the text and of power consists in reclassing it into camps, under the arms of the centurions. Multitude goes from the plebian state to the state of legion, from Quirinus to Mars, from one classification to the other, through an intermediary state that is perhaps primitive. Concepts, units subsuming multiplicities, follow one another allowing glimpses of the underlying *noise*.[1]

~

The partition into classes, the division into three classes is not to be rejected nevertheless. The evolutionist hypothesis did not destroy systematics, nor taxonomy. Classes, genera, families, or kingdoms are still useful. One need only think of them as fuzzy in order to remain sensible, and one need only have suffered exploitation to remain lucid. Moreover, and this seems conclusive to me, the division into three classes, in this case, reveals three universals, three general equivalents, three manners of achieving social essence. The bonds that make for the collective, the obscure general will of whose subject and goal we are ignorant—who wants and what does he want?—this consensus or assent, which is it, or what is it? We do not know, we are stuck, like Jonah, in a black box, and a fluctuating one. What then are we about? The comparatively stable institutions through history are set over the view shafts of this black box. Institutions are based upon a knowledge that they conceal.

We are the sacred, we are the battle, we are the exchange and the money. Each term here is a general equivalent, included in the other two terms, each one is primitive or directly based on the originary. Each one is a social universal.

Each of these universals is related to violence. The sacred shields us from human and global violence, it is produced by it; the military protects us against violence external or internal to the group; the exchange makes our needs flow through channels that, without them, would bring us harm. Violence causes the social bond to be destroyed, it is the war of all against all, so inappropriately named war, the originary war, the social bond is born of its cessation. Like free energy and bound energy. What I have termed a *social universal* is the solution to the question of primitive violence. These solutions, in history, wear out. The most recent to date, economics, is wearing out even more rapidly than the ancient sacred solution or the woeful military one, even if each is still around; the most inspired philosophy in these times would invent a fourth solution, the informational.

Quasi-Objects

That is not all. The only assignable difference between animal societies and our own resides, as I have often said, in the emergence of the object. Our relationships, social bonds, would be airy as clouds were there only contracts between subjects. In fact, the object, specific to the Hominidae, stabilizes our relationships, it slows down the time of our revolutions. For an unstable band of baboons, social changes are flaring up every minute. One could characterize their history as unbound, insanely so. The object, for us, makes our history slow. What is frightening is the inflation of time: things, empires, great men, and goodness knows what else, all reduced to the law of diminishing returns, are passing as fast as the duck at the head of the arrow flying into the wind. The invention of objects, in olden days, froze the frantic flame of relational time to some extent. I have to some extent already said what I thought of the quasi-object, as a luminous tracer of the social bond in the black box. I spoke of the button [button, button, who's got the button?], I spoke of the ball, ludic mimes in our own age of these relational objects. Around the ball, the team fluctuates quick as a flame, around it, through it, it keeps a nucleus of organization. The ball is the sun of the system and the force passing among its elements, it is a center that is off-centered, off-side, outstripped. Every player carries on with the ball when the preceding one is shunted aside, laid out, trampled. Dialectics is almost as lame as the classical sequences when it comes to describing this fluent network. Now each of the universal solutions of which I speak—do you know a human group without religion, warrior, exchange?—forms a corresponding object. Nowhere do I see the sacred without a sacred object, a war or an army without weapons (there are no weapons forged for the war of all against all, no weapons formed expressly for the originating violence), an exchange without values. The object here is a quasi-object insofar as it remains a quasi-us. It is more a contract than a thing, it is more a matter of the horde than of the world. Not a quasi-subject but a bond, not a near-*ego* but what Pascal termed a *cord*, Leibniz a *vinculum*. The social bond would only be fuzzy and unstable if it were not objectified.

The vestals, in Rome, whose relationship to the object I will explain, kept watch over the fire, but above all over the most venerable sacred objects, only the supreme pontiff had the power they had, to know and see them. The secret was so well protected that it has not come down to us. Perhaps it was the secret of Rome's perpetuation. Veneration is the worst possible word in this case, it must be said that such a horror, it must be said that such an absolute terror emanated from them, that it instantly brought any other horror to an end. The monstrance stops the Hun hordes in their tracks, this crude woodcut is simply true in its naïveté. But a cannon would have stopped them as well, this simple image is again true in its crudity. A show of one's weapons is a good use of one's weapons. Contrary to what is commonly supposed, a weapon is made to be presented, like a monstrance, more than to fight with. It is also made to kill, to murder, to cut anyone yielding and taking flight to ribbons. Weapons stop the battle or end it, they are only rarely used for fighting, spectacle or combat sport aside. Weapons are a freezing agent of violence, they are not necessarily its outbreak. Perhaps there has never been a real battle in history, except in narratives of epic and encomium, perhaps there has never been any real reciprocity, exchange of blows, punches, and lumps. The stronger one presents arms and the weaker one runs away. Yes, arms are presented like monstrances. Hiroshima: the bomb ripped up the vanquished and, since then, has been getting displayed. Whoever holds it high halts the greatest violence, how many times, ere? Our history is nought but the time heralded in this question. Here then are the lineaments of our bonds: the crowd prostrate before the monstrances limns a star—the one-all schema. From any given focal point a line leads toward each individual, the group is formed, unitary, what you refer to as power is there. Each time there is power, this star is formed: the center is the potentiality of all; as they used to say in pure geometry, it has the capability of the multiple. It has captured it. Birth of the concept. Powerfulness is just this capacity, the word itself has always said as much. The same pattern emerges if I show or present arms. Fear will freeze all the raying connections into a star and, thus, make them exist. It is still always interesting to find out who is at the center of the star, and I shall attempt to answer this question. Whoever, then, uses a weapon traces the relationship one-to-one, a visible relationship, sword or flame, in the handling of the weapon: this relationship is dangerous because it is shifty, atomic and free, it can drift into the war of all against all. Hence the military institution, hence the initiation it dictates, hence the passage from the monstration of the Celtic hero in a rage hurling his challenge at the opposing hero, to the orderly demonstration of the Roman legions. On this point, I will differ from Georges Dumézil: yes, the hero crosses swords with his adversary, namely the one-to-one relation, but he mainly sets a show going, the thing takes place in front of the lined-up armies. It is a matter of a star-shaped schema, of which the simplest is well traced by the fight of one against three. The passage from Celt to Roman is less a passage from individual to collective than one from a collective in representation to a collective on parade. From the star to the quadrille. From a one-all schema to a schema taking the form of a network. To be continued elsewhere on the same question.

On this network, money circulates, a new object. First it takes on the star schema. In the Roman *census,* each person contributes his farthing, instead of standing still before the sacred object or the combat of chosen soldiers. Each person brings flour or wine to the hero, each pays taxes to the State. Specie or money are in transit in old patterns, and then suddenly, they carve out their own. They go and seek their fortune in the group, and the group is formed by this network. The group exists by fortune, by the goods that circulate within it and go round slightly more freely than in a pre-established network, as is the case with the army on the plain. Money will channel violence, it carries it along and substitutes itself for it. For how long?

~

There are three objects, quasi-objects or pre-objects. The oldest is unquestionably the secret of the chaste vestals, the most lasting is unquestionably the one whose flash we see on the horizon; the simplest and most ordinary is unquestionably in the area of liquid assets. Fetishes, stakes, merchandise. All are objects of desire, terror, and each is sketching or tracing, in the black box, a silent contract. Georges Dumézil's contrast between an individual capitalizing the fury and the legionary order of arms dispersing it in a pattern is valid where money (and the sacred) is concerned: either concentration at a point or circulation. Listen. What then is an object of science? It is simply, merely, an object. An object outside the realm of relationships, no quasi-object or pre-object. It is not at the center of the star, nor on the trajectory of the arrow, nor circulating within the network. It is not a fetish, not a stake, not merchandise. One can even guess what could have been the starting point of this so-called objective knowledge. A thing of no interest, which must have mobilized neither desires nor passions: an absent ideality, a stone falling, a wandering planet. Nothing in that could have become merchandise. It is because there was never any god of gravity that gravity became an object, it was of no interest. We shall see later, in tragedy—in the pure and simple space of our relationships, that is—what an object was. An object of science is the opposite, free, from *those* objects.

As soon as an object becomes a stake, a fetish, merchandise, it leaves the domain of objective knowledge. This makes clear how rare this kind of knowledge is, snatched as it is away from these three fields. Science has shaped another society, quite a different society. When? Where? I don't know, we have no trace of it any more. It must indeed be admitted that it hardly exists any more. That in wanting to replace the society of missionaries, in contracting orders with the society of mercenaries, and in absorbing an expanding financial bulk, science has gotten filled to the brim with fetishes, stakes, and merchandise. Its objects have become fetishes to be worshiped, prize and competitive stakes, and desirable merchandise. Science is returning to the most archaic of societies. It is not science any more, it no longer resolves our crises or our terrors.

~

We will seek another, different social universal. Right away we will have to discover a new object. The money is using itself up, the weapons are at their maximum, the fetishes are dead. I know what the object of science is. But we must find a different object, if we want to survive.

Sacred objects stop violence, for a time only. The vestals in a woeful train conceal them in their bosoms, fleeing a Rome beleaguered by the Gauls. Armies stop violence as well, for a time only. The old terrifying god squatting behind the nuclear flash is rapidly wearing out. Money still stops violence, but also for a time only, for it runs away from it. Inflation has reached the quasi-objects. Can one imagine a different object of science, can one conceive an object of love?

Perhaps our societies, our history have lasted out what these three objects, three schemas, three functions have lasted out. Erosion has filled in their thalweg, it has just finished leveling their mountains. We return to the background noise.

~

When we conceive society, we are missing a decent philosophy of the object. Here the object lies precisely outside of the relational circuits that determine society. In these reflections on the multiple, on the mix, on the speckled, variegated, tiger-striped, zebra-streaked aggregates, on the crowd, I have attempted to think a new object, multiple in space and mobile in time, unstable and fluctuating like a flame, relational.

When we think about society, we are the victims of our images. In the schema of the one and the multiple, the structure goes from the ground up to the rafters. Power belongs to the one perched at the top. Pyramids, skyscrapers, massive cathedrals, towers of Babel—simple, baroque, or complex in their unfinishedness—such are the empires. Gigantic organisms, ogres, gods, animal monsters, Leviathan, their heads reach the clouds and their feet are set on the realm of the dead, like the foundations of immovable structures, such, again, are the major powers or the commonwealths. Complicated flow charts running toward the command unit, vast blue softwares with crossovers and bridges, long brackets embracing the group, these, once again, are the stacks of gray boxes rising toward the sky, like stones, like flesh, here like graphs. The main thing is not the nature, the substance of the model, inert, alive or verbal, as is believed, the main thing is its dimension: its height.

In fact, power digs down. The winner is the one who gets in the most low blows. The king is low or ignominious: limn his lodging in low places, caverns, sewers, cesspools. No, this is not barefaced morality, it is the simple functioning of the law. The social is a sequence, sequence is asymmetrical. The atomic sequence belongs to the parasite, the collective is one-multiple. In order for the sequence to function, it needs a current, circulation is needed on the chreod. One must thus drill downward, lower, to the lowest point. Hence these rivers of Babylon, we weep on the shores of these crumbling rivers. The deeper the thalweg is dug, the more the river, unstable and stable, collects tributaries. The further the main stem flows down, the more its basin spreads out, immense. He who has power over me is positioned lower down than me, this is why my money, my consent, my faith, my desires or hatreds drop down from me toward him, and from my enjoyment or courage toward his gaping mouth. Yes, society forms a sequence, is formed of orderly, asymmetrical, irreversible structures, it thus paves the way for the direction of history, which gravitates toward the deepest shaft. Down.

A weapon is a chreod dug deeper than the eucharist. Many more of us have to bow down before the flash of Hiroshima than did before the host. Our forebears were not more frivolous than we are. Transubstantiation, the sharing of bread become flesh, constitutes the best of the theories on the collective bond, the presentation of arms is a worse theory, but an infinitely more effective one. It is just plain dug deeper. Economics, the circulation of money may ultimately be one as well, even worse than the two previous ones. The fluvial basin of the economy is more general than the first two, it has collected the first two rivers to make them its tributaries. Economics actually says the same thing as theology or strategy, but in a lower voice. It is always only a matter of discovering the one that polarizes the multiple toward it. At the bottom.

~

The comparison between India and Rome, as I've said, is submerged in a positivist philosophy. For Georges Dumézil, and for all of us no doubt, India is theological, metaphysical, and Rome is positive: it is in practice and experience, a matter of history and sociology. The Hindus have remained in the realm of the fabulous, in dogma, they are a matter of philosophy, of mysticism and morality. The distinction between periods and states is acknowledged, in Auguste Comte's thought. And the idea, which is no doubt correct, that decisive progress is due to the group's reflexive recognition of itself and by itself. Georges Dumézil, as a good Roman, brings positive philosophy onto the grounds of our own history. Unless this global dogma comes to us, straight from that very history, our own. Who is behind whom, I don't know who can tell.

Auguste Comte's philosophy, you see, a simple one, and simple because it is only twofold, carries classification, beyond the law of evolution. This encounter is still to be pondered.

Yes, India crystallized around the fixed classes in question, whereas we, like the Romans, seek to forget them, India multiplied the barriers and bulkheads between castes, hardening its social system into a series of closed subsets. Célestin Bouglé didn't put it badly when he said that India had gotten out of history. A proof that history is somewhere other than in classes. India left time, change, evolution, for invariance. This is even a living proof that classification is the optimal solution, if the goal is to stand still. Classing remains a static act: either it is the result of dynamism becoming exhausted or it is the most effective obstruction against a strong flux, to disperse it between baffles, to slow it down, to stop it, to freeze it. Perhaps we must choose, perhaps, blindly, societies do the choosing. Either classing or history; either eternity or time, either the static or dynamism. Just as the classical philosophers used to distinguish naturing nature from natured nature, so shall we also consider a classing principle and the classed group. Some put trust in the moving flux that does the coding and in its process, others put trust in the topography that loses it, in the classifying labyrinth that uses it up. Once more, the same thing can be said again where science is concerned. The more classification there is, the less evolution there is, the more classes there are, the less history there is, the more coded sciences there are, the less invention and knowledge there are, the more administrating there is, the less movement there is.

This situation, so easily grasped that one may suspect it of an excess of simplicity, can pass for a very common one. It happens in knowledge, as well as in history and groups. Either knowledge is lost in the bureaucracy of its institutions, in the complex administering of its own classing, in the multiplicity that could be described as alexandrine or medieval or sophistical or byzantine of its pressure groups, or knowledge trusts in its own inventive élan, but then it tries to ignore, it forgets, heroic, the fractal proliferation of the mouths of the Ganges, where, in the silt and the loam and the mud of the delta, the thread of the water disappears. Elsewhere I spoke of strategy, which is not always, which is rarely, which is almost never a confrontation or face to face, but most often a diversion, a ruse, a topology. Strategy holds the terrain, the paths, the channels, more than the energies. The French language says that rivals dwell on opposite banks, *rives*, they do not run around in the open countryside. They are cautiously separated by water.

Classing is a succession of dams, a complicated arrangement of wickets, hierarchy is semiconductive, the gaps between subsets prohibit crossings, classing is there to disarm, to slow momentum be it creative or destructive, who can tell, to cool down its heatedness or slacken its celerity, complex classing encumbers the bed of violence, or else, since I can't choose, classing is formed by violence and the disorderly course of its flux, violence deposits it as a river lays down in passing its heavy or fine alluvial deposits, it deposits it, codes it, structures it, makes it, it loses some of its virulence along the circuitous route of its products. The gravel comes to a standstill in the flux and, in return, the flux comes to a standstill amidst gravel. Violence makes the classes and the classes unmake violence.

Our three Indo-European classes or functions are so stable in history that they are to be found in the Middle Ages and are there, still, during the Constituent Assembly of 1789, for our picture books. Each of them is a solution to the influx of violence, each class is formed by that influx itself. But the fact that they are classed or form a hierarchy is the major brake on this major flux. Anything can be classed, perhaps, the important thing being to class. The ghastly quicksand-like sinking of our strengths and our lives in administration provides us, these days, with sufficiently weighty evidence of this. Parasitic growth has brought everything to a standstill.

Process

I speak now in several voices. I speak the Darwinian language: yes, an impulse crosses and codes the species. Here are classification, systems, the combinatory manifold at the smallest level, there too is the flux we don't know what to call, perhaps it is life? I speak in the languages of science: we do not know what to call that which codes and passes through the encyclopedia either. Here is classification, specialties and disciplines, the manifold of combinations codes them, there too is history, invention, or the quest for novelty, the fresh force that makes us get up in the morning and makes us laugh at places and boundaries. I speak in the language of history for the group divided into classes. And here again is the division, whatever the principle that does the dividing up might be, and there is the flux, once again, which we do not know what to call. Life, invention, violence, in all three instances, a processual flux codes a classing. We can try to pinpoint this classing, it always comes under combinative art. A method, a certain kind of rationality, analytical intellection unmake, remake this combinatory manifold, as a tapestry is unwoven and woven. But we can attempt to describe the flux and its way of coding, we can also try our luck in following the processual, to see how it slows down everything surrounding its codes. I speak once more in the language of history, processual time and its multiple circumstances pass through the cramped network of their own monuments. All at once, I am speaking of time, of physical time, and the flux is no longer a metaphor, I am speaking of the flux, the laminar flow that is sown, here and there, with turbulence, in which, perhaps, the things of nature are born. I speak in several voices of the sheet of white water flowing along and of the white noise escaping from it that I can hear, I speak of the multiple fluctuations in the flux, I am speaking only of pure process now. It is the time of worlds and things, the time of life, of history, of the group and of knowledge, and in every instance, it weaves combinations either that it undoes, or that slow it down.

One and the same philosophy was able to express, in several voices, classed systems, static, distinct and clear, classifications, analytical or combined, it could articulate them at one go in a language in which old Leibniz was heralding, recovering structuralism. This philosophy is certainly, however, missing the process as long as it clings to the network, the classification, the code, the manifold of combinations. Process as such remains to be conceived: Albula so called before it was called Tiber, the white torrent. Not only does the classed manifold of combinations slow it down as it codes it, but the classing manifold of combinations blinds our conception to the process. To try to think outside of the manifold of combinations and outside of classification, outside of customs and fixed species, outside of discipline and specialty, outside the fossil remains of history, requires living outside of pressure groups and their quarrels as well. The tawdry temptation in life and in thought is still to take refuge in a caste or a discipline, some nook. To become a bird, a shark, a snake, how delightful, how frightful, the metamorphosis.

~

A variant: the most empty and slavish of abject obedience is not obedience to a master, a hierarchy or a ruling class, one may be harshly constrained to these, one has to go on living, it is obedience to the rule that creates this scaled structure of domination, or this hierarchy, these classes, the master, the servant. This law is the competitive struggle to get the carved out places, classed in space, or to form them, constitute them. This struggle creates the classes and the classes create it. Whoever throws himself into the battle therefore obeys, transcendentally. Nothing could be beneath that, in ignominy—except, that is, the one who wins. True independence belongs to the desire for peace. Now this obedience, slavering with desire, most often bows only in the presence of theatrical violence; not of the violence that classes, a fecund and dangerous flux, but of violence between things already classed, frozen into kinds and representations. The great inventive, productive struggles, take place against the current, without any circus or spectacle, and not in the channels of the archipelago, where the surge lies still and stands stagnant, amidst the billowings of slack algaes.

Chaos, Jolts, Mob

To think the surge, to think time, to think process, directly. Let me amend a previous image. I let it be thought that a directional flux produced the coding or entered into the constitution of its graph, I offered a river to be imagined, strewn with its multiple islands. But course and direction are already a constraint. We must go back to the chaos of the ancient, to the opening, yawning wide, to Aquarius.[2] The pure processual is chaotic or, as I put it, cheotic, as well. This latter word leads us back to Aquarius, the pourer-out, the white torrent, the directional. A cascade pours out fairly evenly. Time is a chaos, at first, it is first of all a disorder and a noise. Time is still and always a chaos, a noise, and a disorder. The present, now, is this indiscernible jumble. This chaos is not merely the primitive state, it accompanies my every step, we frequently forget it, frequently it is rediscovered by groups and history. It makes up the great mass of time, its ocean as it were. Distributed, cloudy, and Brownian, as it were.

The different times that I distinguished a little while ago are subject to laws, they are caught in doublets; they pass through bifurcations: time coming down the increasing entropy, the production of minimum entropy, time with a sense of direction, a direction and two senses, and the cycle that has none.[3] This aesthetics is logical once more, and these times are already coded, classed, set in relation to one another. The very images I was sketching: a cluster, a braid, a cloverleaf, in an attempt to think a pluritemporal system, acknowledged only analysis and a manifold of combinations. These are secondary times produced by the chaotic surge. The surge is first—conditional.

~

We must introduce into philosophy the concept of chaos, a mythical concept until this morning, and despised by rationality to the point of being used nowadays only for discourses on madness. When one imports a concept that comes from science into philosophy, one has little bother, all the work is already done. An inspector of finished works, turned toward the past, the importing philosopher, retrograde, is a rationalist at minimal expense. He pockets the fame, the honor, the dividends without ever having paid the price. Cheater. The great hope is to import concepts scienceward, for practices yet to come. Where can these concepts be gotten, these concepts that aren't concepts yet, if not from matrix places, outside of canonized knowledge? Living rationalism is forming into a third kind of instruction.[4] The philosopher is not a judge; if he is a judge, a critic, he never produces anything, he only kills. No. Trying to think, trying to produce, presupposes the taking of risks, the living of one's life, precisely, in the surge outside of the classings of the encyclopedias. Let us then introduce the concept of chaos.

Chaos is open, it gapes wide, it is not a closed system. In order to code, one has to close, in order to class, one has to define, or shut off with a boundary. Chaos is patent. It is not a system, it is multiplicity. It is multiple, unexpected. Chaos flows, it flows out, an *Albula*, a white river. I hear a silky white noise, hardly smooth, with little jumping, jolting bits. A white river would not have any direction or precise bank, it wanders, nebulous. Chaos is nebulous. It does not flow out with a point or a direction, or following some rule, or abiding by some law. Look how much trouble we have thinking it or seeing it. The whole of reason protests—I mean logically. Our whole classified rationality, all the coding, habits and methods, lead us to speak in externals or negations: outlaw and nonsense. But I say positive chaos. Spinoza does not say otherwise: determination is negation. Indetermination is thus positive, and yet we express it with a negative word. I am simply writing the positive concepts of the under-determined, the undetermined, the positive concepts of the possible, thus the positive concepts of time: the nebulous, the blank, the mix, the surge, the chaos, the adelos multiplicities—I mean the ones that aren't obvious, that are poorly defined, confused. Instead of being excluded, rejected, confusion becomes an object, it enters the realm of knowledge, it enters into its movement. And it is classification, on the contrary, that is negative, it is coding that operates in a negative manner, it is the concept, in general, and determination, that is a negation. Our reasoning is negative as a whole, it cannot and does not know how to say yes except with a double no, conjecture and refutation, hypothesis and critique, it is given over as a whole to the work of the negative, and I understand finally why death, so often, is its result, its outcome or consequence and why hatred is, so frequently, its driving force. And why rationalism comes under the heading of the sacred, why rationalists are priests, busily ruling out, cleaning up the filth, expelling people, purifying bodies or ideas. Behold the positive chaos, the casting mold, the matrix. And behold the pure possible.

Let us return to the outflow. When we see a flux, we see a mass, a viscosity, a point, a direction, a speed, in short a mobile consistency. Above all, we divide it up into fraction, and twice over. By sections, perpendicular to its direction: each section must be closed, limited, what would a flux whose sections had no boundaries be, it would, in fact, have no point. Next through what is undoubtedly the most brilliant operation of all time, the differentiation: we get fluxion, or a differential of flux. A fluxion is a fraction of flux as minimally different from the flux as much as possible, apart from size and order. The fluxion vanishes as the flux flows along, fluxion drifts off as flux goes by. The flux is at all points self-coded. Hence the open path from the local to the global. Hence the simplest of methods, open through automorphism. This is our classical reasoning. Let us leave the flowing to the river of forgetting and truth.

Fluxion is a lamina of flux, it is a lamina of the laminar. Fluctuation is a tiny jot of chaos, indeed, a tiny jolt.[5] We do not, as a rule, know how to get from one to the other, from the local to the global and back again, from the chaos to the little jolt and vice-versa, we have no simple procedure at our disposal, in this case, to let us comprehend through concepts. Here again is the pure multiple. Only natural language, Greek or French, for example, can help us a little in these connections, it lets us hear that they exist [*chaos, cahot*]. The jolt is an element of motley multiplicity, it is a jot of noise, like a Brownian surge, an atom of *noise*, a fluctuation of the possible in waiting. Time is at times made up of fluxions, it flows evenly then, redundant, and, already, it is a space. Time is already the space where classes take form, it is already made up of very small classes, it is already completely gridded, it is already frozen. Basic time, close to chaos, is made up of jolts, of fluctuations, it is not integratable, it cannot congeal either in mass or in class, it can't freeze. This sort of time is not primordial alone, or rather it is primordial and it is always there, it never stops being at my side or bombarding me with unexpected jostles, I am always, we together are, we and the world, immersed in it.

~

The Latin language creates a diversion. The *turba* of Lucretius, a stormy mass of diverse elements in disorder, given over to shocks, to impacts, to the fray, a chaos given over to jostling, is a crowd, it is a mob. The physical chaos of circumstances, where the primal *turbo* spirals itself along, is, if I may be so bold, isomorphic with the raging crowd of bacchantes, all set for the *diasparagmos,* or the Roman crowd or any crowd. Chaos makes the same noise as the social mob.

Everywhere we go, we have to go back to multiplicities. For the classed or the classifying life, we go back to a prebiotic soup, a fluctuating mix. Multiplicities: inert ones, living ones, social ones. Can we imagine a chaotic and primal multiple with respect to knowledge, a confused murmur, a *noise* that precedes and underlies the classified encyclopedia? I would like to hear the clamor of intellection in its nascent state, the rage to know.

~

No, history is not born of the divine provinces, that of Jupiter, it is not theological. No, history is not born of the war province, that of Mars, it is not a matter of fighting or competition. No, history is not born of the economic province, that of Quirinus, it does not come from productive labors. It is born of the *noise* from which those three gods, these three concepts, these three objects, these three theoretical classes, these three social groups are born. History is not born of provinces, but of circumstances.

The Work of the Multiple

The real work toward transformation is not the work of the negative, for the work of the negative bolsters the old order, maintains it in its order, and makes time linear. Control confirms the role, a counterforce protects the force, and none is so conservative as the teenager who has grown old, outgrown his rebellion against the father. We suffer as much from governments born of revolutions as from those that backed us into them. We suspect them of driving us to it to be able better to maintain themselves, under a second facade. What is called dialectics is a rather crude trick of the straight line's, a logic of carefully placed invariants.

The work of transformation is that of the multiple.

~

In the beginning are the meteors. It rains, snows, hails, blows, thunders, and the fire of heaven passes. In the beginning are nameless words, verbs without nouns. Stone is bombarded by the unfurling of the wave, its crazy lace is the memory of the undertow: this fractal complexity is a trace of the multiple, the real multiple, different in every aspect. The soft dune is blown across by the sand, the earth cracks and breaks up in ice, the cloud dissipates in the midst of turbulences. All things are worn away by the mighty crowd, erosion is caused only by large populations. The immense tide of the multiple makes, unmakes, it passes, destroys or constructs, we do not know, blocks up channels, seals off ports, opens new paths, levels the contours or exaggerates them, cleans space out or peoples it with clouds of the upper air: to speak of these transports as positive, negative, is mere naive anthropomorphism. The multiple moves, that is all. In the beginning is the multiple: it rushes around.

The crowd goes by, dispersed. It rushes around, like a torrent.

~

Thus, the weather, meteoric time, qualified as fair or foul, is in precession over the time that elapses, passes, comes round again, starts over or flies.[6] The wear and tear, the erosion, the breakdown or the embolus, may mark the stages of the temporal *temps,* but they are made up of the meteorological. Climatic *temps* precedes and makes temporality, the time of organisms, clocks, systems, the time of precipitations is the driving force of these temporalities.

We must praise a language that has a single word with which to gather these things together, receive them in the same ensemble of meaning. The *temps* of multiplicities, of those large populations in disorder constituted by storms, winds, snow, and clouds is thus close to those temporalities of a partial, reversible or irreversible order, as if the latter were born of the first kind, shapes against a background. Orderly temporalities stand out, can be read, knit together, against the background noise of the climate. We must praise any language that associates meteoric clusters, hail, hurricane, turbulence, squall, with the Greek word *climate,* which means: inclination. Yes, the climate depends upon the place, the place is defined by an angle that has reference to the equator. But I am tempted to see in this climate the inclination from which the time of order is born, making its appearance, a circumstance, amidst the clamoring disorder. In any case, climate is an aggregate concept, statistical and multiple. *Temps* is an aggregate concept, when it means atmospheric conditions, it is a simple, unitary concept, when it means length of duration counted by the clock, by an organism or by any given known system. The latter is on the side of the one and the foreseen, the former is multiple and hard to anticipate.

~

All things are transformed by fire and time. The time of erosion and wear would not happen without the weather, without the bombardment of winds, sand, atoms, without the knotting nodes, and the turbulent tresses of comet-tails coming untangled. A few ordered times are born of the disorderly time.

Fire is no differently the work of the multiple. It may be destructive or artistic just as the weather can be fair or foul. So what? Heat, a scientific concept, has no dimension, it is a statistical concept, Cartesian, it also subsumes disorderly multiplicities. Heat surrounds the multiple in fluctuations, like atmospheric conditions. Heat is a concept from the scientific era, what it covers is none other than the mythical concept of chaos. Heat is our chaos. Heat-cloud, chaos-cloud, when it comes to the disorderly motion of molecules. Chaos-pourer, heat-pourer, when it comes to the motive force of fire. Indeed, there is work only under the immense thrust of the multiple. Fire is a shaking up of myriads.

~

Time-as-weather, fire-as-heat are not concepts in the usual sense. Clock-time is such a concept, entropic time is, perhaps, another such, and temperature as well. A cloud is an aggregate, a nebulous set, a multiplicity whose exact definition escapes us, and whose local movements are beyond observation. A flame is an aggregate, as I have said, that is even more nebulous. Here then are a couple of concepts in which the multiple reveals itself as such. Heat and flame, cloud and wind, climate and turbulences, we could refer to them as concepts for multiplicities.

We are, now, well enough prepared by our sciences to be able to conceive them in their unanalyzable complexity. They are epistemologically possible. Nature makes us live in phenomena of this sort, you see. Language describes many areas of mixture where the multiple is gathered without necessarily being sorted through some unitary wicket. It is not an everyday occurrence when there is a potential meeting between refined branches of knowledge, overt phenomena, and everyday language.

From now on, we can conceive the multiple as such. We need it in the humanities and social sciences.

~

Philosophy does not have the exclusive duty to think what the sciences think in the way that they think it. It can do so at its leisure, but then it must clearly recognize that it is, depending on the circumstances, being slavish, parodic, a parasite, a copyist. One may well wish to become a copyist or to live as a parasite, it's even a comfortable existence. One may get a laugh from a bit of parody, as well.

Philosophy does not have the exclusive duty of being separate from science. It can be, at its leisure, but then it must clearly recognize that it is, depending on the circumstances, an ignoramus, an historian, confined to the institutions that are its own. One may well wish to exhume corpses. One may shed a tear at this sad occupation, as well.

There is no philosophy without the sciences, there is no philosophy within the sciences. Philosophy thinks with them, but outside of them.

Philosophy tries to think what the sciences do not think, what they do not want to and cannot think, what they sometimes forbid, what they keep one from thinking, what they are not yet thinking, what they have forgotten, what they have covered up, what they do not know how to project. It keeps as its most precious possession a freedom of thought that the sciences, in their procedures, can never allow themselves. To be a philosopher is to know how to regulate this liberty as it is to be able to liberate oneself from regulations.

The sciences amongst themselves perform a surveillance, a monitoring that is both conceptual and social, and which defines the validity of a learned procedure. Consensus is the ensemble of these monitorings. At a given time, the community knows, as though instinctively, what is admissible. To be learned is to have this knowledge, often without knowing it. This regulation, this self-regulation, this set of feedbacks in the network of relations, makes up the main constraint for anyone wishing to enter the community in question. This is the cost of efficacy, of all efficiency: as much for discovery as for honors, medals, and careers. We can imagine a scale that would allow us to weigh real efficiency, objective, primary efficiency, and establishment efficiency, the secondary, social efficiency. The dominant theories at present say that no such scale exists, since competition is the driving force of discovery. These hypotheses are too favorable to those currently in power to have any hope of being plausible. I can imagine a scale of that sort. And I think science has been getting off on altogether the wrong foot for two or three lustrums now, in having more and more in common with some social group or other and less and less with its founding characteristics. The monitoring in question works only for monitoring, only for selecting, the maintenance and perseverance in existence of a group that lays itself open to becoming a pressure group, slowly ceasing to be fruitful. In other words, the scientific community is in danger of arming itself less to ensure discovery or invention, than inventions are advertised in order to ensure the status of the scientific community. Once that happens, the monitoring, in rational procedures, becomes a social constraint on thinking more than an exercise or ascesis with invention in mind. This is happening, right now, throughout the scientific and scholarly institution, everywhere within the university. Free thinking is put in danger through the working of the strategies of fine thinking. This is the reason that, unfortunately, the sciences so easily line themselves up under the relentless tyranny of bureaucracy, under the idiotic despotism of administration, in that silly bovine subservience to politics. Reason in the null state, known as reason of State, is driving out reason in an excited state, as bad money can drive out good. The working of the monitoring of intelligence can become—oh irony of ironies!—not at all unlike the slowed-down dynamism of stupidity. And little by little the masters of the institutions of the mind mimic the masters of violence, their heads adorned with horns, their snouts snotty with base imbecility and torpor. Will I live to be old enough to see science, my last hope, become beastly stupid? The same adventure must once have befallen other scholars, the same disappointment must have flayed other lively hopes.

Philosophy is only performing its regular duties when it drills us in liberation. There was a time when science liberated us from certain slaveries and from darkness, there was a time when this discourse of circumstance was quite simply true. Sadly, the time has come when the sciences are letting themselves get trapped in the customary subservience of groups who are looking only to perpetuate themselves as a group. Thought can only live free from these constraints. The misfortune of our times is that these constraints are precisely those of thought as such: exactitude, rigorousness, precision ... Hence our narrow margin, our small degree of freedom: thinking with scientific thinking, but especially thinking outside of it, knowing how to free oneself from these stifling regulations, but also knowing how to regulate this freedom. Inventive reason has before it but the eye of a needle to be able to pass through, freedom tempered by rigor.

Intermittences

Once we had order to conceive, new orders to construct. Then we thought through structures, with the sciences, but outside of them. The counterfeit money, in those days, was printed without the sciences, but by mimicking them; already it was driving out the good. And then we conceived order under its broadest and most powerful category: a structure is, in a sense, an ordered multiplicity of ordered multiplicities. It moves far-off aggregates closer to the broad expanse of the welkin, but provides them with a rule or a procedure that operates everywhere in the same manner. Thus, new orders have appeared in unexpected places, the social sciences, literature, the history of religions, even philosophy, have been able to participate in the algebraic festival of structure. With it and outside it.

All this, of course, presupposed aggregate thinking, meaning thinking in multiplicities, which had always been lacking in philosophy right from the start. The structural effort implied distribution. The message being exchanged passes over the background noise. Twice we found ourselves in the presence of the multiple. Three times even, since we must count fire, heat, Zola and Turner, the irruption of huge populations in the thermodynamic oven. Just as structure is the broadest and strongest order ever constructed in the history of knowledge, the multiple as such seems at first to be pure disorder. It is precisely as loose in its dissemination as structure is extensive in its network, an ultra-long-range construction on top of fluctuating myriads. This pure multiple is the ground of order, but it is also, I think, its birth, or at least its power in the sense of potentiality. Perhaps real work only happens beneath the thrust, the shift, the fluctuations of the multiple. Bundles of prospective circumstances obliterated in the void or vanishing in an order which forgets them.

The mob fluctuates and the institution is made of stone.

~

The universe is intermittent, it is quasi void, it is a distribution, a sowing of nebulous forms, clouds, galaxies. Was it originally dense and continuous? Possibly. Today, it seems to be an immense fractal turbulence, a global turbulence of large, medium, small...

microscopic turbulences. The universe becomes, in an intermediate state, ordered, to be sure, disordered, assuredly, and almost everywhere empty.

This model has huge ramifications, like countless models at work in our knowledge today. Certainly we had never had any concept of order more extensive or comprehensive than that of the cosmos. The cosmos was the order and the universe was in order. It was our refuge, our security, our roothold, the most far-reaching and surest foundation of our living habitat. Those who did not believe in God, as the guarantee of their existence and their righteous thinking, thought, or sensed, vaguely, beneath their thought, the order of the world. The classical God of philosophers and scholars was in fact nothing else but this rational guarantee, this university of reasons and laws. In this sense, the most religious, the most theologian-like of the men of the world is the contemporary scholar when he puts his trust in that old universal order. And most often such a man calls himself an atheist. The cosmos was thus the foundation of the house and the condition for knowledge. Order reigns, all quiet, our science and our confidence.

It is not so; our earth is quaking. The cosmos, the universe, in our languages, are misnomers. It is better seen, ultimately, as an intermediary, it is a mix of order and disorder.

Solids, Fluids

Once, I put forward the simple idea of different states of metaphorical matter. I had noticed it in Auguste Comte, where the supposed law of these three states follows very clearly the three states of matter—gas, liquid, and solid—then distinguished: the world itself was formed according to these three stages, and the history of human beings came into line with physics. The idea itself is explicit in Bergson's thought, in retrospect, it sheds light on our regular misconstruals of Lucretius, and the road down which these misconstruals have misguided us right up to the present. In other words, our metaphysics, metaphorically, feels the effects of our physics, it feels keenly the effects of the privileges granted, by our science and by us, to this or that state of matter. Our world is solid, our earth was solid and our heaven was as well, we too are secure, everything is in place around us. The very request for a foundation, for existential or gnoseological foundation, implies that one does not dig or lay a foundation in water or on the wind. Bergson is thus right to say that our metaphysics are metaphorics of the solid. The solid, then, is nothing else but the unit of multiplicities, a unit applied to or found by or for a large population. Thus, a concept is a solid, and the solid is almost already a concept. We were afraid of gases and liquids, we understood nothing in Lucretius, our knowledge was not made for the great multiplicities.

This old classification of solids and fluids is no longer very interesting, we are more inclined to conceive ordered states on the one hand and disordered ones on the other. We are still so foolish—meaning so full of fear. We were afraid of wind and waters, we are now afraid of disorder and the rarely predictable. In fact, we are afraid of multiplicities. We never want to conceive multiplicity as such. We run away from this thought.

The solid is the multiple reduced to the unitary. A concept is a multiple reduced to the unitary. A representation is a multiple reduced to the unitary. Any power is a multiple reduced to the unitary. The strength of the State is another multiple reduced to the unitary. The history of the crowd redistributed into camps, in Livy, and of the massive withdrawal of the plebs shows how history, politics, and spectacle negotiate the multitude to conceal it beneath a simple law. We run away from the throng, fly before the scattered distribution, before the aggregates, under wind and waters, flee the clamor, and we cut our losses and leave the rest to the mercy of the flames.

Bergson believed that it was necessary to make an effort to go back from the solid to the liquid—from space to time. All of this is too hastily put: space is dense with flux as well. To go from solid to liquid is only a matter of heat, one must therefore increase the disorder. As for time and space, I have spent enough time elsewhere showing that the question was much more complex, there are many kinds of spaces, perhaps even as many as you like, there are also a few kinds of time. The effort consists in going from the one to the multiple, from the ordered state to the disordered state. But disorder is the worst word imaginable, it is here only to induce pathetic reactions, be they learned or unschooled.

I prefer to call these two states, unitary and multiple. The one is a gathering, and the other a distribution.

To say disorder is to say that one is both unwilling and unable to conceive it. It isn't an anti-order, perhaps it is a more exquisite order still, one our banal stupidity cannot manage, stiff as a board as it is, to conceive, since it is still given over to concepts—to order.

This is why I have first tried to conceive the turbulent state. To do so, I have had recourse to Lucretius's poem about nature and to Immanuel Kant's theory of the heavens, the two philosophical monuments, one ancient and one modern, on the question. That the cosmos appears turbulent to us, today, seems to me to be true, inevitably, to the state of things, that it is fractal, intermittent, appears just as pertinent. What is turbulence? It is an intermediary state, and also an aggregate mix. Assuming that we distinguished the disordered state from the ordered state, turbulence is a medium between these two states, it is a state, difficult to conceive, difficult to study scientifically, but at the same time a common, widespread, all but universal, exquisite state in which there is an order, an inchoate or a final order, and in which disorder and chaos are also to be found. Chaos appears there, spontaneously, in the order, order appears there in the midst of disorder. We will assuredly, some day, have to abandon this so negative label, disorder, which implies that we are thinking only in terms of an order. The turbulent state mixes or associates the one and the multiple, systematic gathering together and distribution. System appears there in the distribution, and disappears there, distribution appears there in the system and disappears there. Hence, the forgotten philosophical tradition that described, with precision, nature—the things themselves at their birth, at the moment of their birth, in and through turbulence. Turbulence is an intermittence of void and plenitude, of lawful determinism and underdeterminism. It is an intermittence of being and nothingness, an intermittence of several reasons. In this area, the least error as to the initial position makes for an immense uncertainty as to the final position, after a chain of even middling length. Here, determinism reigns, there, underdetermination fluctuates. Here, classical science reigns, there, the new tree of multiplicities fluctuates. Here, time is in legal expectation, there, our uncertainties waft along on forecasts, in the meteorological sense. There really are two different sorts of temporality, Newton's time and the weather outside, we return to our premises, but climatic temporality plunges into the multiple, Newton plunges into Democritus.

Turbulence is a mix of foreseeable regions and chaotic regions, a mix of concepts in the classical, unitary sense of the term, and of pure multiplicity. Turbulence is a multiplicity of local unities and of pure multiplicities. Just now, I was defining structure as the largest and most powerful concept of order that the history of thought has ever encountered: an ordered multiplicity of ordered multiplicities. It was the largest of the world's orders. Now we confront the basis of this form: a chaotic multiplicity of orderly or unitary multiplicities and chaotic multiplicities. A philosophy that has conceived structure must conceive distribution, or better still, turbulence as the broadest base to this broad form. A philosophy that has conceived structure and turbulence must conceive the multiple as a concept that is common to this fluctuating background and this stable form. A philosophy of communications conceives the message as order, meaning or unit, but it also conceives the background noise from which it emerges.

~

Turbulence is widespread everywhere, almost everywhere, yet it is not universal. There are turbulences everywhere, but not everything—far from it—is turbulence. Leibniz used to say, likewise: there are monads everywhere, but not everything is a monad. There are units everywhere, he would say, there are multiplicities everywhere, we must say. The twisting smoke, the torrent, all of a sudden, strangulating itself, the slow mixture, stately in its indolence, of liquids scrolling round, the torquing avenues of eddies along the river banks, a flurry of wind, a string of irregular squalls, the wake of rudders and airships, the throbbing pulse of blood in the vessels, the clouds overhead and the clouds of Magellan, yes, turbulence is widespread almost everywhere, in the inert and the living, in nature and technology, the infinitesimal and the cosmological, and perhaps my body, my corporeal-order, my corporeal-disorder, life and death, perhaps it is after all, it too, only a temporary turbulence, linking up smaller turbulences, in a unitary, though ramshackle, fashion, whence contingency, circumstance and the individual. Everywhere, almost everywhere, there is turbulence, but not everything is this intermittent multiplicity. It is a strewn phenomenon, distributed multiply in space and time, it is not a universal phenomenon. Gravity, fortunately for Newton, is universal, heat is universal, fortunately for Fourier, magnetism was similarly the good fortune of Maxwell ... Turbulence is intermittent, in its very definition and in its presence, in its nature and in its distribution. Multiplicity, before reaching unity, or without unity, has gaps, it has margins, it is riddled with exceptions, it is in tatters. Turbulence is not universal, and yet the universe itself is turbulent. The cosmos was an order in its designation and its reality, similarly the universe is thus named to show everywhere, without any lacuna, the reign of a single rule. In every direction, toward any point, and whichever way any observer turns, nothing new will appear, just the sun of this law. Such is the universe where gravity is concerned, it is *univ*erse when it comes to heat; but it is diverse when it comes to turbulence. The universe is opposed to the diverse: let the observer turn round, something else appears to him, unexpected. Everything happens as if there existed a concept of totality with regard to a phenomenon. We must definitely give new names to the world. With regard to attraction, it is a universe, with regard to interactions, it is one as well, with regard to heat, it is endowed with universality, perhaps, but with regard to turbulence, it is, if I may put it thus, a diversality. Turbulence is diversal. The world is empty here and full there, sometimes being and sometimes nothingness, here order, there chaotic, here occupied, there lacunary, sporadic, and intermittent, as a whole, here strongly foreseeable, there underdetermined, here temporal and there meteorological—here, I mean, predictable or reversible and there an estimate and aleatory, here universe, there diverse, here unitary and there multiplicity, all in all when all's said and done a multiplicity. The cosmos is not a structure, it is a pure multiplicity of ordered multiplicities and pure multiplicities. It is the global basis of all structures, it is the background noise of all form and information, it is the milky noise of the whole of our messages gathered together. We must give it a new name, definitely: it is a mixture, tiger-striped, motley, mottled, zebra-streaked, variegated, and I don't know what all, it is a mix or a crasis, it is a mixed aggregate, it is an intermittence. The most global concept, by good fortune and freedom, is not a unitary one. Order is never more than an island or an archipelago. In the midst of the multiple, one finds universe-isles.

~

Phases are phases, they are not phases alone, they are models of knowledge. They are not solely objects. A cloud is cloud, it is not solely an object. A river is not just an object, neither is an island nor a lake. Likewise the noise of the sea. As I proceed further along, a harmony is taking shape, unexpected. The phases, gaseous, liquid, solid, the clouds, the river, the jagged coastline, the plateau, all of them express par excellence a given mode of knowledge, they construct the world I am in. I can imagine the point at which the description of phenomena and that of knowing will knit together. The world carries in itself its gnoseology. It is no longer incomprehensible that the world is comprehensible.

Old Empedocles foretold that the physics of Hatred alone had made the objects of the world obstacles to be overcome, gotten around, masked, pulverized, destroyed. Objects are objects, objects are models of knowing. The world is full of the working of knowledge, as they used once upon a time to say that it was singing the praises of God. Perhaps we shall enter the second Empedoclean phase.

Mix

Let us once more take the sayings of the Ancients seriously, too hastily prejudged as prescientific. The demiurge of the *Timaeus* forms the soul of the world with three materials: the same, the other, and a mixture of the same and the other, he mixes these three elements into a single unique whole, and then he divides them up with harmony, and then he composes this dividing up into a cross. Plato uses trickery the same way we use trickery with the unthinkable. The trick is superb, and there is thinking for you! Plato is intelligently supple and our dogmas are stupidly stiff. Yes, knowledge, science are on the side of the same, invariants, stability, and the one. That isn't at issue, who disputes it? This having been said, the philosopher might refrain from indefinitely traipsing over and over the same, or else make himself genuinely learned. The hypocrisy of the philosophers of science is to claim that one must be learned without ever truly being so themselves. So then, what is there outside of knowledge? I do not know, might as well call it other. This other that science rejects, that it doesn't know or doesn't wish to know, that it will perhaps know one day—but what difference does it make?—this other known elsewhere as either disorder or chaos or chance—but what difference does its name make?—this terrain outside of thought, outside of the thinkable, outside science, is not dogmatically rejected by Plato, but rather he tolerates it, negotiates it. Yes, philosophy negotiates the unthinkable. Science remains within the same, and spends time marking off the boundaries of the other, but the philosopher is a demiurge, and his object is the other as well and the same as well. Should he mix them, he then is really a demiurge, and Plato is, consequently, the demiurge itself. He tolerates that other that science does not tolerate, he even mixes it with the unitary. From the thinkable and the unthinkable, I say, he makes a third substance difficult to conceive. The same and the other, and this book knows something of this, require force to be able to be mixed together, so resistant or loathe are they to mix. The demon works even harder, he mixes the three elements, the third of which is the mixture, in doing so giving a great priority to the mixture—the third term. See how he uses trickery, how crafty he is with the unthinkable, how he negotiates the unavoidable presence of the other. He negotiates it, you'd think he was domesticating it, taming it, he thinks it. He does not exclude it, as we do, for he knows it will return, in any case. Our pure clearcut reasons have been crazy for ignoring these returns. From this mixture, I say, he makes a single unique whole, and in doing so he gives priority to the same—to the first term. Then, he divides with harmony, through proportions and *mediatae*, always giving priority to the same, the similar, science, then he cuts out and crosses and again finds the other... Plato's ruse, the ruse of the demiurge manufacturing the world is immense and powerful, it's our own ruse here: we are attempting to think within the concept and outside of it, we are now thinking an aggregate, it is nothing but pure multiplicity, but it is an aggregate, but it is riddled with holes, lacunary, sporadic and thus multiplicitary, but it is a unity of local unities and of scattered multiplicities, but... For the *Timaeus*, the world is a harmony, the world is a mix, the world is unitary, formed, composed, thinkable, but it is mixed only with mixtures, it even is a mix of mixes of mixes, but... The ruse goes on, and Plato pulls to the right to the one-ward, then he pulls to the left to the multiple-ward, then pulls to the right again... and so forth. What he means by this, what I mean by this, is that we must think on the side of the thinkable, that we must tack toward science, toward the same, toward the one and stability, but that we must then be ready to think the unthinkable, that we must then change our tack, toward the pure multiple, we are continually tacking back and forth, the method being a fractal meander, to one side for safety, to the other for freedom, to one side for the regulation of our thoughts, to the other for boldness and discovery, to one side for rigor and exactitude, on the other side for mixture and fuzziness... This is philosophizing, this is how we were able to pass from one ocean to the other, the passage fringed with ice and landfalls to the waters of the northwest. Plato is a master in the arts of navigation, his world a mix of the same, the other and a mixture of the same and the other is both thinkable and unthinkable, mixture of thinkables and unthinkables: and so science becomes possible and it succeeds, and so science explains the world through series or polyhedrons, and so in a relay with science, myth goes on, and in a relay with myth, science... Philosophy, demoniacal wisdom and science, is endlessly weaving the two languages, the demiurge itself is mythical, and yet he helps out in mixing the clay of series... we now know that myth is so good and so profound when it comes to anticipating our social sciences that it can sometimes be more knowledgeable than our sciences themselves and that our sciences, in return, so full of myths, can be in the dark... Here then unity winks with multiplicity, in the elements as much as in the work itself and in the discourse that articulates this work, here, I mean in this very page and in the *Timaeus,* the same blinks on and off with the other, flashes and occultations, science with myth, presence and absence, matter and void, order and disorder, general turbulent intermittence, as dots, dashes, and blanks blink, the ones immersed in the others, in a message to be decoded, as this message winks with the background noise that carries it and that intercepts it, that brings it to us, that hinders it and that prohibits it... the world is this very immersion, thought, messages are these immersions, distributions in systems, systems immersed in distributions.

Time

The customary, I hardly dare call it ordinary or basic, experience of time is that it, at times, is composed of instants, and that, at times, it flows by, devoid of units. It is discontinuous and it is continuous. It passes and it does not pass. It comes back on itself, sometimes, and, sometimes, it lapses or is lost, absented. More than present, through this redundancy, and more than vanished, in its lability. Time becomes expansive and contracts, all at once dense and soon spread out. Full, empty, intense or flat, vertiginous, banal, cut quite lengthily by an abrupt fault, uniformly full, blank continuously. I am not describing events, exceptional or bereft of contour, or these or those brief or lengthy circumstances, succeeding one another in time or constituting its sequence, I am telling its texture of being and the way that it passes. It does pass and it is. Time is lacunary and sporadic, it is a badly stitched tatter, it passes, loose, a mosaic. Time is a pure multiplicity.

At times...at other times, sometimes...occasionally, this is what language can say, at most, of its distribution. Either...or else...this is what it often cannot say about it. Because time, at first, doesn't choose or sort, doesn't filter or eliminate. To do so, it would have to be equipped with bars or edges. It therefore imports and acclimates within itself all negations, it receives into its bosom, positively, the indefinite of all determinations. It encompasses even opposites and contradictories, which has wrongly led people to believe that contradictions are the motive forces of time. In fact, what never was can happen with time, what can no longer happen was able to be. I saw in the days of my youth things that seem impossible to those making ready days when I shall not see incredible things. Time is the positive infinitude of possible determinations. It is the omnitude of novelties.

Time is not, as a rule, a line, although it may become one, and then start selecting, sorting, eliminating, getting all at once bushier and bushier with bifurcations: another time on top of time, appears; time, nonlinear, is, most often, a sheet or a field.

Might it then be reducible to space? or to a space? Let's get this straight once and for all. Space is what we call a relatively homogeneous, isotropic multiplicity, subject to some law or a definition. It is always necessary—perhaps it is not sufficient, but it is at least necessary—it is necessary to have a certain redundancy in order for a space to be, in order for a space to be thinkable. Now, while time can manifest, at times, some repetition, it is a multiplicity with minimum redundancy.

Basic time is a tatter, a patchwork or a mosaic, it is a distribution, through which, at times, redundancy passes. A multiplicity marks and shows some redundancy, it becomes spatial when this repetition increases. Should it greatly decrease, then time appears.

Language, once that happens, is suddenly bereft of possibilities for eliminating. It cannot put anything outside or inside a boundary, it cannot draw a boundary. Without redundancy no path, no edge, no outside or inside, the adhesions waft and the proximities fluctuate.

Time is a tatter and it is sporadic. It solidifies like a crystal or vanishes like a vapor. It is an unintegrable multiplicity, endowed, here and there, with unities, there and here deprived of snapshot moments. It is not a flux that can be differentiated into tiny little fluxions, although it can become one and then become fringed in differentials, it is, for the most part, a sumless aggregate, a bundle of dispersed fluctuations. It is not a set, although it can become one, it goes in bursts.

~

Supposing it is possible to conceive, in the most abstract way in the world, a universe of possible multiplicities, I assume it would be possible to arrange them, according to the amount of redundancy or repetition they involve. Let us imagine a god who could give himself over to the quantitative analysis of their redundancy, he would spread out before himself a continuous spectrum of multiplicities. On this spectrum he could detect a place, a kind of threshold, with null redundancy. No multiplicity, at this place, starting from this place, on the left, would entail, make manifest or make known any repetition. Pure chaos starts here. The *noise* is there, noise, I don't yet say fury, so repetitive is fury in its stupid way. Moving down the scale of redundancy, multiplicities descend into chaos.

Starting from this null threshold and outside of it, in its vicinity to the right, multiplicities fall into line where redundancy increases. We can imagine a point at which this redundancy, though not nil, would be minimal. At this point, basic time appears, the time I have described. Only slightly repetitive, it is repetitive, at times, simply in not eliminating the possibility of repetition. To its right is unfurled the continuous spectrum of spaces.

Space and time do not make up a pair of notions, unities, forms, or sets. Time, in the sequence of spaces, is the subdeterminant of redundancy. Make redundancy increase slightly, and an order begins to be born, you enter spaces. Spaces are thus multiplicities that are slightly, somewhat, considerably, extremely ordered: at the maximum limits of redundancy, totally ordered, like the space we call Euclidean, homogeneous and isotropic.

Time is a threshold between disorder and redundancy, it is the multiplicity next to chaos and prior to all spatialities. It is the first injection of redundancy into a pure multiplicity.

~

Let us come back to the painting of *La Belle Noiseuse*. Neither Porbus nor Poussin discerns anything in it, for lack of redundancy. The pure multiple is not recognizable in any of its points. The first of the redundancies is marked by the space of the foot. It is the lowest of the redundancies, it is, rhythmically, its unit.

What is a process? Process is a step or a dance, an advance. Process is a procession. Indeed, it is necessary that one of them begin, lead off with a step or get off on a foot. Time is a process. Basic time prepares the process. Here is disorder, here is chaos, here is the patchwork of badly stitched tatters, upon which there appears, locally, a first process or the beginning of a process. In order for it to pursue its sequence, it will certainly have to have some repetition, it will have, in some way, to go from a first step to a second step. And so forth. It then enters a time that is to some extent reversible, already assimilable, or reducible to a space.

The canvas, then, will enter the realm of painting, it will enter representation, it will enter into the sequence of spaces. It will enter redundancy.

For the moment, it manifests time.

~

The *belle noiseuse*, in an identical manner, is temporality. She flows like the Scheldt [like *l'Escaut*].

See the whirlpool eddying upon the river, it is the first step of things.

~

It is easy to specify the minimal redundancy, the initial repetition, incipient dawn above the waters of chaos, it is the echo. The rumor is at hand, the echo repeats it. Languages like to articulate it in various ways: tohu-bohu or brouhaha.

When a fluctuation appears or forms, it is never a beginning, not a sowing, it is just one of the myriads, of *noise*, indistinguishable, incapable of differentiation. It is a sōwing only if it is or has an echo. When Leibniz, toward the end of his life, wanted to link the monads one to the other, he clearly understood that the echo was the atom of harmony, as the elementary link. The echo in the valley brings back to Robinson Crusoe, alone on his island, the voice of his soul, the verse of his soul; it does not repeat the name of God, proclaimed at the beginning. All of the fluctuations dispersed in the background noise are incapable of differentiation, undifferentiated, as they await a frequentative.

~

The *noise* is incapable of differentiation, everything in it is indistinguishable. It is laminar and white: each lamina takes the place of any lamina, white noise, continuous aquarian outpouring, sustained noise of waterfall, a null signal, formless background. It is a saturation of differences: the cloud chaos returns to the aquarian chaos for, shall we say, a complementary reason, no signal will pass through the innumerable plurality. The indistinguishable returns to the continuous, the continuous returns to the indistinguishable. No difference or complete difference both produce the undifferentiated. The sense of hearing is lost in silence and also in pure noise.

The *noise* is the fury of all against all, we do not distinguish the names, the faces, the weapons, nor the hate nor the mad wrath of the raging men face to face, we don't distinguish the faces, there is no face to face. Fury is as white, it is as total a difference as a cloud or an aquarian outpouring.

Let me make clear that the observer is shot through as well with sound and fury. He does not soar above the waters.

~

I begin again. A fluctuation appears, it is lost in the desert or the packed-fullness of background noise, either through lack of reference, or through excess of difference. It vanishes, it gets buried. In order to be or to make an appearance, it needs a reference, it needs an analogy. It is either set in the laminar, then, or it is distinguished through its identity in the differentiated. It thus needs an other, it needs a same, it needs an echo. The echo alone is discernible here. Either through its position or through its redundancy. In the beginning is the echo. Background noise, fluctuation, echo. Everything begins on the threshold of the echo.

The echo is the minimum of redundancy, then, sown in pure multiplicity. Time is born with the echo, the echo is from birth to make time begin.

~

The sense of hearing perceives the echo, tohu-bohu or brouhaha, a double fluctuation, the very first seeding upon the cloud or the white noise.

~

In the beginning is identity, the principle of identity.

In the beginning is imitation.

Mimesis is to the humanities and social sciences, face to face combat or competitive desire, what the principle of identity is to the hard sciences.

They both are varieties of the metaphysics of the echo. They both are varieties of its prelanguage.

~

A crisis is a return to the multiplicities. Evidence that the multiple is possible, that it is open to the future. What is in crisis returns to basic time, suddenly losing its gel of redundancies or relying on what I have referred to as the omnitude of novelties. Dying to be sure, being resurrected elsewhere, at another moment, unpredictably. The multiple in question is not a relay, or it is a relay with utter freedom.

~

Here is some invariance, here are some stabilities—stupid, heavy, even, odd, standing there: statues, sandbags on the ground. Here, more subtly, is some invariance by way of variations: this top remains all the more upright and firm on its axis the faster it spins, just about the same thing goes for the terraqueous globe, the system of the world, and others. Here are some more intelligent invariants, caught up in the movement itself: the river flowing down remains in equilibrium all along its bed, it can be said of it that it flows steady; I am growing old and I am changing, alas, I resemble myself. Constancy must be looked for at the heart of instability.

I am looking now for an invariant, blindly seeking a new stability, a secret one, perhaps unheard of. I am no longer speaking of variations, fall or circulation. I am speaking of those transformations, to call them volatile is an understatement, without apparent law, that are produced by the irregular bombardment of circumstances. I notice them in the inert world and in life, history or culture. Everywhere multiplicity brings about the metamorphosis of things.

Of course, things would not be there, existing, knowable, I would not myself be here, alive and voluble, without some constancy. There must consequently exist some oneness in and through the multiple. I am attempting to articulate the principle of reason.

Is the theme still audible beneath the quite meticulous bombardment of the melodic line, beneath the *noise* of background noise? It shouldn't be audible. This should no longer be left standing since this storm of sand has been blowing up in its bursts. We should no longer be here, so formidably does hatred go about its work. Well, the world is still here, beneath the meteors, the living is perpetuated in the storms of the multiple, history goes on in its nauseous bath, I still hear meaning in the pandemonium. Must there be a reason for the perpetuations of these existences? Does there exist anything stable enough, quasi invariant, in, through, in spite of multiplicities?

~

Turbulence is a median state between a slightly redundant order and pure chaos. It is a state of birth, a state of nature, in a temporary state. It also is a death threat.

Turbulence spins, on itself. Here and there its motion is reversible. It is born in the time of clocks, of planetary systems and intimate atomic vibrations. We know reversible time because we are positioned in a steady region of an immense turbulence.

Turbulence is born of the *noise*, it is born unitary, to some extent, it takes shape. It takes shape, rises up, anadyomene, before breaking apart in the noise. It passes from pure multiplicity to something of a unity, it is in a time generating newnesses, we thus are acquainted with this time from being alive in a new region of a turbulence.

Turbulence is not unitary everywhere, nor totally ordered. It collapses here and breaks up, it passes locally from the one to the multiple and from message to noise. It thus runs along the time of entropy.

Turbulence is the form of synchrony at three different times, a form I had described without being able to refer to it except as a cluster, a ringing of changes, a cloverleaf, looking for metaphors for want of forms. Turbulence is the fragile, original, elementary, everywhere present form of the interexchange of the three redundant times, the three space-times, the three times endowed with unity. A repetitive unity, a formed unity, a unity undone.

Turbulence rises, anadyomene, above basic time, a tatter with a minimum of redundancy, a multiplicity bereft almost of unity.

It is the first form, it is the first tower.

~

One must imagine Venus turbulent, above the noise of the sea.

Dream

From the depths of familiar, ancient traditions, strange objects come to us.

An ingenious, intelligent, organized, articulate, and sedulous people undertakes to build. The Tower of Babel will reach the sky. Near the end, however, the project fails and it fails, so it is said, through a confusion of tongues. In the desert there will remain some stones, a whole gigantic ruin slowly split and slaked by waters and wind, mastic trees, goats, frost.

They fell apart, for lack of comprehending one another, after having had such a good understanding. The stones are scattered now and brambles pass through the walls. We want to understand this text, we want to understand the tower, we want to understand this people, we want to understand this us, this people that constitutes this work and this tower. Let us undertake, then, to comprehend this collective aggregate. Ingeniously, intelligently. We draw up plans, blueprints and graphs, flow charts, we construct a system, we even conceive a general theory of systems, a kind of general, universal system for reaching the sky. Let us call this whole endeavor the constructivist model. Now then, it ends in *noise*, in the foreign noise of external languages, soon spoken by the enemy. War, fury, the system lies in ruins. Upon these rocks no one has ever built anything but Babel. Babel is not a failure, it is at that very moment when the tower is dismantled that we begin to understand that one must understand without concepts. Here and there, Babel is unified, a few great stretches of bare wall appear and remain, colossal cathedrals, half-swamped in the rubble, monumental temples overrun by the jungle and its chattering apes, vertiginous twisted paths on huge slopes, there and here, Babel, collapses in noise. Babel is an unintegrable multiplicity, a sort of intermittent aggregate, not closed upon its unity. Together we are this strange object, immersed in the clamor. At times constructible, here and there, and yet not totally constructible. We are this tatter of languages fringed with murmuring. A tower plus noise, a system plus *noise,* tremendous architectures of walls, plus wailing walls where the moans, groans, and weeping can cleave the stones already loose. Then, we understand. History begins.

~

If the tower was not finished, it was because this industrious people constructed it, back in those days, with stones alone. They did not, as it is said, have the means. Men are not stones, no community can be built in this manner. Living stones are needed for it. You are Peter, then, and upon this rock I shall build. Let us undertake, then, to construct or comprehend. Ingeniously, intelligently. Cell by cell and life upon life. Let us call this entire endeavor the biological model. Here is that massive, colossal animal called Leviathan, or 666, a Babel in flesh and fleece. We are not really sure if this organism is viable, we only know that it is monstrous. Good, evil, I do not know, misshapen in every instance.

Leviathan or 666 are animal towers of Babel, weird live objects, weirdly formed, shapeless. The people who build Babel try to understand each other and really do understand each other only at the uncrowning, through confusion of tongues, of the finishing pinnacle. The collective is not an architectonic, or, rather, it is an unfinished architectonic surrounded by noise. The monster is, in animal manner, a variety of Babel. From living beings born of living beings we have only ever seen living beings. Never any societal creature.

The frog [in La Fontaine] explodes with a loud noise from having wanted to be the size of an ox. That was only a slight error. Anybody can build a pyramid, a tower, much higher, broader, taller than the little pyramid of Mykerinos. Just look at the pyramid of Cheops, it almost succeeds. But a frog the size of an ox is an ox. Some adjustment is needed, then, in the course of growth.

Swelling, inflation, homothety ultimately, are not enough. The frog, quite clearly, doesn't know this. It only makes a minor error. But when the fabulist brings princelings and their ambassadors into his moral, when he sneers at the marquises and their little pages, he causes his point to swell as the frog did, he moves from the barnyard to the courtyard, just as the little tree-frog went from a frog to an ox. And his error is greater, for he enlarges his apologue even more, in size, number, and relations. Again we must understand that we need to understand without using concepts. This world full of people who are no wiser is a frog the size of an ox, plus the noise of the bursting, plus the envious fury of the frog's sister.

The monster is inconceivable, but it is faithful to the real. 666 is repetitive, cancerous like the frog and its metastases.

~

Yes, the constructivist model is promising, but it provides only bricks and mortar whose final product is unattainable. Yes, the biological model holds promise, but it begets only monsters, it opens up a teratology of unclassed animals. It remains for us to meditate on the unfinished.

The tower is unfinished because it was built with stones, we are not stones. The animal is monstrous because it was formed of living beings through a thousand ingenious experiments. We are not living beings alone, we do not in any way live like animals, our cities are different from anthills or termitaries, our towers are not beehives. We construct with concepts, with ideas, we build with illusions, the imaginary, sudden awarenesses, representations and even recently via information. Our Jerusalem is made up of software, cities of God, bailiwicks of the Word, megalopolises of language exchanges. We are making ready for the kingdom of the spirit, the celestial Jerusalem or a classless society.

Wait, then, for the end of history to see the realization of the promise rise up at last. Passing from hardware to software, the material to the logical, the tower of Babel turns over, and with it the point of its text. In the old days, lack of completion used to come in whenever all was said and done, never had the end been so clearly in sight. Nowadays, incompletion is the ordinary state of affairs, synthesis and unity finding themselves asymptotically relegated to the inaccessible furthest reaches. The noise, once upon a time, and the fury were obstacles to the end of history, the terminal setback to construction. We changed all that: the *noise* is here, it never stops, our whole life we are subjected to furies and noises, Babel being infinitely removed, displaced to the time when the whole gamut of times will end, to the moment when the sum, the summation, the consummation of the ages will come to a close. The incompletion is common, and we shall inhabit the great pyramid only when we are dead. Perhaps we only really know how to build tombs.

~

These crazy traditions have wisdom—ruins, monsters, and dreams. What they say is as simple as ABC: in history and the social sciences, definitions are not closed, concepts are not formed, that in these matters incompletion is neither residue nor failure, but state of things. Many are the places there where people believe, where, above all, they make people believe, that one can understand through concepts, that it is possible to construct and finish construction, from the foundations to the rafters, to develop, from the cell to the organism, that it is possible to deduce or relate otherwise than as a fool or player, that to dominate and anticipate, in theory and practice, is done by being clear-cut and axiomatic in closure, whereas there is always only a multiplicity. Institutions seem always to be founded on this lack, situated on the narrow slit from which the incompletion could be seen, they obstruct the opening in shadow, and crown the misrecognition of this cognition. Their cornerstones are rolled in front of the tomb or the entrance to the underworld. Like Ulysses or Aeneas, the philosopher must at least once in his life, enter in and go down, speak to the obscure shadows that cannot take shape, and rake over the ashes. And he must avoid being seated on the stone and carrying on the discourse of the deaf establishment. It would seem that power has the role and function of making people believe that both concept and reason, closure and domination exist, where there is only ever pure multiplicity without any unity. Ruins, monsters and dreams, and time without redundancy—these always come back, in spite of the crude endeavors of these machines to transform the noise and fury into all sorts of order, discourse, harmony, sense of history, architecture. We are ceaselessly trying to repair the not very reliable machinery that is there to make the confused noise gel and the fury crystallize, but the *noise* exceeds its capacity. The *noise* is more powerful than its mechanical force. I mean: incalculable. I mean: measureless. It always exceeds the machines' capacity for calculation. Yes, politics weaves together the rational and the irrational, but this tissue, rational, is ripping apart indefinitely, it is a tatter.

~

I imagine a hard nucleus surrounded by clouds of the upper air, I see an island, a mountain, I see an archipelago scattered in the midst of the clamorous sea, a jagged mass beneath the snow and in the clouds. I imagine a set of distinct objects, pieces, sections of Babel, immersed in the confused murmur of tongues, walls penetrated or covered with viscous fury. I imagine the clear bathed in the confused, the distinct overrun by the indistinguishable. I see flashes of unities amidst occulted multiplicities. I hear messages that rend the haze with the noise of their pointed and barbed overlap.

This, which I see and hear, which I imagine, is a theoretical and abstract landscape, a model of knowledge. And this, at the same time, is nothing other than the world.

~

I am building a tower and I have no name for it.

I once saw the tower of Thales, the translucent pyramid in Egypt, pierced by sun and intuitive epiphany, a flat projection space growing from Mykerinos into Cheops and even beyond, to absorb the spaces of the world and of thought, I have not forgotten the scope of the shadows, nor the death upon which the tomb is built. I saw the inaugural tower of reason, half of it black, its foundation of ashes. The tower of Thales is perfect, it is transparent, it is mute, it is a tomb.

The tower of Babel, imperfect, is immersed in the noise of the tongues.

I saw the tower of the Leibnizian *Theodicy,* an infinite pyramid. Its peak is a perfect apartment, the best of all possible worlds.

There is the culmination of harmony. The noise, in this optimal spot, is as faint as it can be. Yet there has to be a bit of it, that grain of salt, that minimum, that false seventh chord which renders harmony sublime. When harmony is pluperfect, it has noise as a prerequisite. The Leibnizian pyramid lets this smallest noise be heard at its extreme peak, the apartment slightly lower than the best of possible worlds lets a louder noise be heard, the further down from the top toward the wide base one goes, the worse are the possible worlds, their harmony, music and peace, decreases, the *noise* rises. The tower of the *Theodicy* plunges down and takes root in a confused virtuality, one probably need not go down very far to be steeped in senselessness, mounting clamor, and raging hate. The pyramid emerges from the noisome, nauseating flood, it emerges from the deafening noise and its peak alone is at peace. Rational optimism is a boundary, I was going to say an exception, this world is a beautiful musical stroke of luck.

Could the tower of Thales the geometer be only the last apartment of the pyramid of possible noises?

Could the tower of Babel, uncrowned above by the haze of languages, be the very pyramid of the ˉ *Theodicy*, upside-down? Here, in the vicinity of the apex, harmony is a major value and maximal, sound and peace, there, noise and fury forbid anyone getting through.

Boundaries are terrifying or peaceable, and the body of the work is confused or orderly.

～

This shows that the *noise* is always ordered when it is not eliminated. It remains in its place and does not exceed its bounds. The excess itself cedes. Harmony is increasing or decreasing in inverse proportion to the noise and the fury: multiplicity enters into the unitary law. The tower of Thales is a pure order, even if it is set on a corpse, the Leibnizian pyramid an ever purer musicality, even if it is visited by a condemned man, the *noise* is relegated: either to the foundations or to the other worlds. Or rather: let us abandon the tower when the *noise* of the tongues comes up.

It is always assumed that multiplicities can, through various procedures, be eliminated. I assume that they cannot be, I find that they cannot be and I hope that they are not. I assume that they cannot be, metaphysically. I find that they cannot be, scientifically. I find that they cannot be, in technology. I hope that they are not, in deontology and politics.

The construction of the tower is a new rationalism.

∽

I am slowly getting close to it. Not so very long ago, I constructed a Kantian pyramid. Born of the *Theory of the Heavens,* this tower does more than just reach or touch the sky, it comprehends and occupies it.[1] With intelligence, it mixes systems and distributions, unities governed by laws and scattered multiplicities, local organized worlds and chaos in the manner of Democritus. It does not eliminate chaos, it welcomes it and acclimatizes it. The universe is a mix of hard nuclei and high clouds, archipelagoes and seas, flashes and occultations, messages and noise. The distribution is basic, it is originary, it never stops, like the background noise. The pyramid is built of strong unities and multiplicities, just as an ordinary construction is made of cement and sand, stones and sand, iron, sandstone, glass and sand. Why eliminate the sand? The mixture, you see, is so skillful that it becomes, in its turn, an order. The tower's design manifests lines and alternations, sequences and laws, infinite nestings. The pyramid has internal homothety, like a Von Koch curve, the former, of course, is the source of the latter.[2] And the mixture is so intimate that there is no chaotic or distributional place, above or below, right or left, not surrounded by systems, and no system place, left or right, above or below, not surrounded by distributions. The elementary link in the construction takes the following twofold form:

	D				S		
D	S	D		S	D	S	S = System
	D				S		D = Distribution

just as if the main concern was to border disorder with order and multiplicities with unities. These neighborings are so refined that the interpenetration is total.

This vision of the world is a fulfilling one for me. It is intelligent, subtle, deep, precise—faithful to the things themselves, faithful to our ways of knowing. An abstract landscape, a model of knowledge, the spectacle and unfolding the world—all of these at one and the same time. We have only ever had pure precision silhouetted against a background of mist, we have never seen a compact system that does include within it a kind of pool of confusion, we have never heard of rigor without noise.

As far as the above diamantine form with the fuzzy edges and the other, ringed one, this island and this lake, go, like Kant, I do not think that they are articulated within a legal network, a regular system, a pyramidal tower, I believe they are strewn in a sporadic jigsaw puzzle. This mutual immersion, this bathing of islets of order or negentropy in a fractal sea of commotion, lakes of noise in a formerly glacial soil, this bathing is not endowed with regularity, it is itself a distribution, it is a pure multiplicity. Or rather, we do not know, as a whole, whether the world is itself a unitary system or a lacunary multiplicity. I propose the hypothesis, on which Kant must have paused awhile, that the universe vibrates between the one and the other, that it never stops pulsating from one boundary to the other, from a homothetic tower in which the apex, the point, is a system, to a homothetic tower in which the apex, the point, is a multiplicity. God never stops undoing himself into gods, and the gods are continuously unifying themselves into God. To be is the pure risk of Being and Nothingness.

I think and I go astray. I think and I flutter about. I am I and one alone and just barely a plurality. The way I think and the way I am is no different than the way the world pulsates. I do not know in any other way. I do not speak in any other way, I take the pure risk of logos and chaos. The word gleams in the dark shadows and the dark is at the heart of knowledge. The purest and most rigorous knowledge includes some obscurity, some magic, and incompletion, there are gold veins in barren rocks. At times, information, numberless as the sand, overwhelms and invades me; at times, a lightning intuition of some arrangement takes hold of that crumbling dune and a cathedral appears. The multiple is in me and in the world, turmoil within and racket without, without our being able to establish the edge where these noises meet, the unity of the I is wakeful in me, harmonic and constant, the sense of things, obvious, is in front of my eyes, unitary. Order and disorder, the one and the multiple, systems and distributions, islands and sea, noises and harmony, are subjective as well as objective. Now I am a multiplicity of thoughts, the world is now as orderly as a diamond. What fluctuate are the order and disorder themselves, what fluctuates is their proximity, what fluctuate are their relationship to and penetration of one another.

~

I am attempting to extricate myself from the hell of dualism. Utterly pure rationality is a myth, it is a sacred place, cleansed, purified through lustral procedures that expel the confused, the profane, the unclean, the victim, accordingly, excluding, in any event, for the greater glory and power of its new priests. Everyday rationality is religious, in an archaic sort of way; conversely, everyday myths often contain the seeds of reason. The opposition between science and what is not science, what is thus obscure, senseless, demented, falls at once into anathema, into schism or heresy, the history of our sciences looks so much like that of our religions that it's hard to tell the two apart. Armed struggles between pressure groups, reason, and right are too often on the side of the victor.

Science is not necessarily a matter of the one or of order, the multiple and noise are not necessarily the province of the irrational. This can be the case, but it is not always so. The whole set of these divisions delineates the space of the *noise,* the clash of these dichotomies overruns it with its noise, simple and naive, repetitive, strategies of the desire for domination. To think in terms of pairs of separated elements is to make ready some dangerous weapons, arrows, darts, dovetails, whereby to hold space and kill. To think by negation is not to think. Dualism tries to start a ruckus [*chercher noise*], make *noise,* it relates to death alone.

It puts to death and it maintains death. Death to the parasite, someone says, without seeing that a parasite is put to death only by a stronger parasite. Keep the noise down, says he, without perceiving that he has monopolized all the noise, without understanding that he thus becomes the head of all the fury. It never ends, sadly, soon a harsher thunderclap will come up behind him. The purest is never pure enough to remain the master forever unless he turn his reason and his right into those of the mightiest.

Love is not the opposite of hate, for hatred is the whole set of contraries.

~

The pure is in the impure and the obscure is in the clear. We live and think within the mix. Zebra-streaked, tiger-striped, variegated, motley, fleck-speckled, bedizened, star-spangled. We invent, we produce like the Demiurge, in and through the mix. Here are two men, the one who transforms and the one who criticizes, the one who picks the chestnuts and the one who sorts them, the one who roasts them and the one who tastes them, the one who produces them in the trees, the soil, the ashes, the fire, and the one who judges them, sitting around indolent; why should reason always be on the side of the parasitical judge? Critical rationalism stages a grand courtroom scene, the producers make do with what they have as best they can. Glory, for once, to the inventor, glory to the inventive philosopher. A young Kant invents, invents the heavens. The heavens, then, are constellated, a right and true thing, a systematic star is edged with black distributions, a black hole of chaos is surrounded by crisp stars, an intelligent model of constellations, a motley model. The one is in the multiple and chaos is in order. The immense pyramid rises, it carries chaos all over in its synthesis, as if the architecture were everywhere packed with the confusion of tongues. Noise is needed for messages, sand is needed for stones, how much disorder is necessary for living beings, how much noise is necessary for history?

In his old age, Kant proceeds to the court of justice, he installs a judge, he criticizes. Now multiplicity is only there to be unified. I'll leave him. And plead for invention, and I am not pleading before the court of critique. We need exigency, we hold that there is need of a strong exigency, who's denying that, but we must not leave the monopoly of the rule to the sterile critics and the power of the impotent. Kant constructed the theory of the heavens, I'm not talking about Kant any more. But you who judge, you who wield critical exigency, you, what have you invented? What have you done except recopy? If you had gotten your hands dirty, you would no doubt be aware that there is some dirt.

~

I am not building a tower, I see a kind of city rising, I am not altogether building, it is making itself, I'm taking part. Here are a thousand pyramids and thousands upon thousands of spires. These delicate arms, cilia quivering in turbulence, are born of the low white fog, these here, an infinite number, fade away, they break up, though they will return aperiodically, others rise higher only, once again, to disappear, those there gel into an edifice, steeples.

I remember the slapping of the waters in the Sargasso Sea, and how in that remote retreat of a place there were those dancing bottles. Each message trying to raise its voice to some extent above the maritime *noise*, it only gets through by reason of the rise of the swell, it falls back at once into the trough and the noise, a carillon that is piercing and cacophonic with the fluctuating collisions of glass. Can a boundless hallelujah come of it? A hallelujah that isn't the swelling of a local echo?

~

Our thought, our understanding, our life, our masteries would just be foolish and simple if they maintained ties only to an orderly world. And the world would be stupid if it were so. Redundancy cannot be the master of things, we may as well say that we are happy among rocks and the dead. We still do not know all of what comes into play, secretly, in the inmost reaches of crystals, the rocks are not entirely rocks. We may as well say that we are happy with the repetition of death. Order is the unit of the multiple, it is thus redundant, it can be lethal. Indispensable and dangerous.

Order can be simple or complex, so they say. Its complexity does not change things very much, it is the name given to the simple when it seems new and impressive. Complexity just takes some time and a bit of work, the time necessary to reduce it to the simple and for it to come to look simple. At first, the eye is lost, the ear is uneasy, the intelligence flutters around. But one always ends up by undoing the tangle of hawsers, eye-beckets, bights, overlappings, a network is always just a knot. Because he was young, Alexander was in a hurry to cut through; because Ariadne was young, she was Theseus's impatience. If there were only labyrinths to get through, we would not have to get up so early in the morning. But the Classical Age, or rather the Baroque, has already said all there is to say about complex combinations and the time it takes to bring patent multiplicities into hidden unities. Happy age when the simple, in style and thought, sheltered or held tight the complex, unlike the sorrows of these times in which the complexity on display conceals only simplicity. A network is always just a knot, a signal is just a sum of waves, a complex is always just a simplex.

~

We maintain relations with things without relation. Our thought, our understanding, our life, our masteries, everything comes into play here. The perceptive bursts, the turbulent environment, the circumstances and accidents, the unexpected intuitions, the news, the dangers, ultimately, the arrows that flieth by day, they keep us awake. If we are requisite, upright, alert, tensed—if we are alive, it is because we know, because we hope that the unforeseeable will happen, that it will be unconnected to what is already there or already assembled, that it will catch us off our guard and that we will have to negotiate. Encounters in the middle of the crossroads, drama, luck, change of course. Life and thinking die and lie dormant from a lack of events, advents, adventure, a lack of history. If history took its orders from one or a few laws, we would be reduced to what we think the brute animals are. We understand nothing of origins and beginnings because we are drugged with order, we dream coiled up in the woeful security of our complexes.

You are afraid of your anguish, you rush to exchange it for your money, so it will be comparable with and measurable by the general equivalent, you are afraid of noise, of this *noise* rising in the silence of our organs. It writhes, howls, breaks loose, insane. Keep the noise down: health is just this silence. Wrong. Maladjustment, uneasiness, the rumblings running through our quiescent body are already, often, guides to life. In killing this parasite, smothering the nascent clamor, in being afraid of our own tears, are we not making the same blunder as in eliminating the confusion from clear thinking? At times vagueness is a sign of invention, sometimes pain can be the beginning of change. The most precious thing we have, the most precious thing about us, are those shifts that shred us to bits, thrusting our adaptability forward and off-kilter as it were, putting it at risk, in jeopardy, in danger, in torment for the sake of making richer existence and more festive our knowledge. I am in pain, therefore I change. We often call pathological that which should guide normality, that which pulls it out of the ditch in order to enrich, diversify the solutions. Sadly, we distrust life's unexpected resourcefulness. But what if, quite to the contrary, this conservative and attractive point where we are contented in morose delectation, this place at the bottom of the well of equilibrium, were the pathological place? Here every rift is reduced to zero, here every call produces silence, every project rubs itself out. Health is not silence, health is not harmony, health deals with every appeal, every cry, the caterwauling; from a meagre old melody, me today, weak, ignorant and craven, plus the clamor of circumstances, it creates a magnificent new orchestral display, its *oeuvre*. Health never stops beginning. It is seeking a chord that is powerful, coloratura, warm, brassy, plentiful, amid the tearing and terror of the *noise*. Yes, anguish guides life and anxiety heralds the new. Without thinking, we produce the unexpected, our hope, and danger, our enrichment.

~

Let us imagine again a set of scales, scales of beings or intelligences, as they used to say in the old days. Arms rise up, quivering cilia, like tiny spires. Let us imagine that the noise rises, the *noise* increases as we go along these unities, along these orders.

Health is not silence, nor equilibrium, if it were it would just be the little death of corpses passing by, chilly, pallid, translucent. Health negotiates the *noise*. The noise increases. Health, in a tizzy, forces itself out of its torpor. The *noise* continues to increase. The body follows, what does not kill it, makes it stronger. The *noise* is still increasing. The body invents heroism, transfigured solutions. What volume of noise and what height of fury can it accommodate before it collapses, ashes to ashes? The athletic and the adaptive individuals have poked around at the threshold of this scattering of ashes, they are survivors. Every living being is a survivor.

Listen to these violinists: the one who lets true musical harmony be heard is the one who gets close to the brink of catastrophic noise, he pokes around with his bow on this threshold. He is stirring up the flame in which the rosin would melt.

Thought in activity is not order, deduction, or purity, if it were it would only be the little death of the repetitive copyists. Thought sets its foot on the hard nucleus of rigor and redundancy, so as to go further afield, the *belle noiseuse* weighs down and alights, she crosses the blazing torrent, she looks for another rock on which to set her other foot. Thought negotiates the *noise*, negotiates the unexpected, it moves instinctively toward the unforeseeable. There is no new thought except Aphrodite born of the waters. She advances, she invents, collapses, gets a foothold on the rock, courageously advances: the rocks are strewn about haphazardly. Her stride changes in length, angle, rhythm. The *noise* increases. Invention follows. The *noise* continues to increase. Invention grows stronger, it can become sublime. It knows it wouldn't be anything if it indefinitely reproduced the unity. There are cases where the repetition of order breeds cancerous monsters. Invention is ceaselessly negotiating multiplicities diversely increasing. What farflung and diffused power might it not assume before collapsing in babblings? Philosophy, dangerous, heroic, is poking around at this brink, visiting this threshold, pitching its nomadic tent there. It would return to science or the tradition of the always already there if it got scared of this nearness, it would take refuge beneath the protection of what the *noise* calls the major currents of thought. But philosophy is an anticipator. A little too late and it becomes a historian, a copyist, a parasite, or, worse, it fights under somebody's colors. It can anticipate only by giving itself over to multiplicities.

What boundless tide of useful and accurate information is science itself going to be able to integrate before tumbling into barbarism, carried off by that awful tidal wave of articles? Science receives, science produces this bombardment, it negotiates it. It is easy to see in this case how the *noise* is external and internal both. It can happen that science is its own *noise* with itself, it produces its noise from itself, to the point of not being able to hear any message, and its own fury, through a hundred thousand conflicts between subfaculties, to the point of no longer being able to reach any agreement. This is the everyday state of a quite ordinary Leviathan, warned by the honks of its own geese of the noise of the approaching enemy. The body, thought, knowledge, the collective, history not only negotiate an extrinsic *noise*, microbes, confusion, enemies, multiplicity, they produce an intrinsic one, through the very process of negotiation, and the labor of negotiation. Often, all you have to do is fight an authority to become inflated with it.

~

The noise and the fury are interred beneath the transparent tower of Thales the geometer, at the foundation of our knowledge. Noise and fury are the signals for the cessation of work, on the Tower of Babel, all have abandoned the unfinished pyramid. Tomorrow will be heard the noises of the cathedral sucked under. Noise and fury are brought to a minimum at the harmonic pyramid, the tribunal of the *Theodicy* rescues God from the suspicion of evil through whittling down to a minimum the *belle noiseuse*. The multiplicities must keep quiet. Protagoras, the empiricist, is six feet under, with his vortices.

Immanuel Kant sows the heavens with noise and fury, he tries to reconcile Democritus and Newton, the knowledge of chaos with the order of the diamond. The tower is built with sand and stones, with bursts and concepts. It crumbles and it lives. The more it lives the more it collapses, the more it collapses the more it lives. It lives because it collapses, and gets bigger by dispersing itself. The sand of multiplicity marks the end and the beginning.

No. There is no tower, there is no integration, there is no hierarchy, no level, not even a rule running through time instead of being built in space, no overrun or replay, no structure of order in general. It can happen, however. There do exist, to be sure, orders of things, but multiplicity does not serve as a relay, it is, it remains a multiplicity. Here are a few orders, then, scattered, steeped in the multiple, in noise, in chaos. Necessity glints there by flashes in the contingency, one hears its message amidst the confused noise. Here are some orders, each in its order, prey to the growth of the *noise.*

The degree of fury and noise that a living organism can deal with, that a device, a piece of equipment, a technical apparatus can process, that it can tackle, that a science integrates, assimilates, comprehends, that an art blends into its putty or its marble or its language of sense, that a culture accepts, that it expresses, that it produces, that it accommodates, that a political system tolerates and lets alone, for the sake of freedom—this amount, this dose, if it were measurable, would tell the excellence of the organism at the top of the taxonomy, this living being speaks out rather than take refuge in the redundant order of instinct, it spreads out every which way, it deals with the sudden gusts of circumstances, it has an unstable history, this dose would tell the suppleness, the power, the refinement of the technology under consideration, hardly any noise in a lever, a bit of noise in a clock, the topography of a motor is already designed in relation to the chaos in the boiler or the cylinder, the distance that separates mechanics from the living is a distance of contingencies, of handling unrelated multiplicities, of a flexible grip on turbulences, of return to equilibrium, after an incident, via unpredictable paths, this dosage would tell the subtle progress of science, the overt refinement of a civilization or the sublimity of a work of art, would tell ultimately, would tell above all the simple happiness of living as a commonality in the heart of such a city, the subtle pleasure of inventing, within the plurality, one's own conduct, one's own language, one's own individual work and private existence, one's body itself.

Existence or excellence lies in the fringe, it is on the edge that never stops; it is in the bath in which things are immersed. See it emerging from the waves, listen to it.

～

I do not know who it was that said that one does not write initially with ideas, but by making use of words. That is such a shallow thing to say. In the beginning is not the word. The word comes where it is expected. One writes initially through a wave of music, a groundswell that comes from the background noise, from the whole body, maybe, and maybe from the depths of the world or through the front door, or from our latest loves, carrying its complicated rhythm, its simple beat, its melodic line, a sweet wafting, a broken fall. One cannot grip one's pen but this thing, which does not yet have a word, takes off. In the beginning is the song. Language is not the subject, it is still less the infra-subject, why bother with this useless reduplication? The words then easily take their places along the line of this volley or the lines of this volume, even the strictest mathematicians know that one cannot invent or demonstrate anything without the coming of the secret and right harmony of the notation. Then the musical wave embraces space:

does it drive away the fury? does it wipe out the murmuring? I do not know, I know that at times it steps aside, painfully negotiating the *noise*, spreading somewhere else, forming a new space still unknown to the squabbling, it invents a blank space, out of the shouting, out of the hell, where it can lay out its peaceable feasts and its fragile truth value, before the noise shrouds it in night. Under the word and language, this wave, and beneath the wave, the black *noise*. The unknown, the infra-subject of hate and multiplicity, open chaos, and closed simply under the numbers. At the seeding of the wave and the surge, as at the beginning of the world, is the echo of pandemonium. The word will be its messiah, and the idea will be the messiah of the messiah, awaited in the noise, hoped for in the raising up of the musical renaissance.

Notes

The Object of This Book

1. [Throughout, Serres uses the archaic French word *noise*, which would be unfamiliar to many modern French speakers or would only be known to them in the phrase *"chercher noise,"* meaning "kick up a fuss" or "look for a fight." Serres discusses the connotations of the word in the first chapter. In general, it denotes "ado, strife, contention" and thus ties in with, but is distinct from, both the concept of auditory "noise" and the scientific and information theory concept of "noise" (both of which correspond to the French word *bruit*). In our translation, we have consistently rendered the word *bruit* by "noise" and have indicated when Serres is using the archaic French word *noise* by putting it in italics. Needless to say, no parallel situation exists in English.—Trans.]

Chapter 1

1. [L'Escaut is the French name for the Belgian river usually called the Scheldt in English.—Trans.]

Chapter 3

1. [Matamore is a stock character in many seventeenth-century French comedies; originally found in Spanish theater, he is a *miles gloriosus* figure, i.e., a blustering, swashbuckling braggart and a loud-mouthed bully whenever he can be; his name derives from Spanish elements meaning "killer of Moors."—Trans.]

Chapter 4

1. See Serres, *Rome: Le livre des fondations* (Paris: Grasset, 1983); *Rome: The Book of Foundations*, trans. Felicia McCarren (Stanford: Stanford University Press, 1991).

2. [In French Aquarius is *le Verseau*, literally the pourer-out of water.—Trans.]

3. See Serres, "Espaces et temps," *Hermès V: Le passage du nord-ouest* (Paris: Minuit, 1980), 67–83.

4. [See Serres, *Le Tiers-Instruit* (Paris: François Bourin, 1991).—Trans.]

5. [In French, the global chaos sounds just like the local jolt: *chaos, cahot.*—Trans.]

6. [In French, a single word refers to both time and the weather: *temps.* Serres here proceeds to distinguish between the two kinds of *temps.*—Trans.]

Dream

1. See Serres, *Hermès IV: La distribution* (Paris: Minuit, 1977), 123.

2. See Serres, *Hermès V: Le passage du nord-ouest* (Paris: Minuit, 1980), 101.